MUSKRATS
AND
MARSH MANAGEMENT

The Muskrat being itself. Photo by Jim Sherman, Iowa State Conservation
Commission.

MUSKRATS

AND

MARSH MANAGEMENT

By
PAUL L. ERRINGTON

A Wildlife Management Institute Publication

University of Nebraska Press
Lincoln and London

A contribution of the Iowa Cooperative Wildlife Research Unit, Ames, Iowa. Fish and Wildlife Service (United States Department of the Interior), Iowa State University, Iowa State Conservation Commission, and Wildlife Management Institute cooperating.

First Bison Book printing: 1978

Most recent printing indicated by first digit below:

1   2   3   4   5   6   7   8   9   10

Library of Congress Cataloging in Publication Data

Errington, Paul Lester.
  Muskrats and marsh management.

  "A Wildlife Management Institute publication."
  Bibliography: p. 177
  1. Muskrats.   2. Minks.   3. Trapping.   4. Wildlife   management.
I. Title.
[QL737.R638E77   1978]   639'.11'3233   77–14177
  ISBN 0–8032–0975–4
  ISBN 0–8032–5892–5 pbk.

Bison Book edition published by arrangement with The Wildlife Management Institute.

Manufactured in the United States of America

PREFACE AND ACKNOWLEDGMENTS

Like so many other north-central youngsters, I first became acquainted with muskrats in the course of prowling about the countryside. I learned that they had salable pelts in cold weather and that it was not too hard a job to separate pelt from the rest of the animal and to profit to some extent thereby.

Fur trapping became a major source of livelihood for me during youth and early manhood, 1915 to 1928. Although I regarded myself as a professional trapper, I never strung out large numbers of traps nor covered wide areas by dog team, horseback, motor car, or aircraft. My practice was to operate carefully on a somewhat local scale.

Apart from winter-long experience in the Cheyenne River drainage of western South Dakota and in the Big Bog country of northern Minnesota, most of my trapping was done on the Oakwood-Tetonkaha chain of lakes and marshes and along the Big Sioux River of east-central South Dakota.

While muskrat trapping, itself, took a relatively small proportion of my total fur trapping time (my "specialty" being mink trapping), it still could be for me a highly important seasonal pursuit. It might require day and night concentration for a week or so each year while the trapping was most profitable and competitive, or it might be spread out over a month or longer when and where less hurried exploitation could be carried on. It was done mainly in December and January, which, at South Dakota latitudes, often meant sub-zero weather.

* * *

My years of graduate study, 1929-32, were relatively muskrat-less and so were the first two years following my appointment to the faculty of Iowa State College in 1932.

In 1934, still at Iowa State College, I had an opportunity to center professional attentions on muskrats again, in beginning long-term investigations of these fur-bearers and their living requirements and ways of life. (See the section on selected references given at the end of the book.)

These investigations dealt little with muskrats in cages. My principal objective was to learn about free-living animals in environments that were typical of north-central United States and adjacent Canada, to learn about animals living if they could and dying if they had to. I seldom interfered with this living and dying unless information might be gained through interfering.

Some of my interference in the private affairs of north-central muskrats took the form of experimental trapping to test trapping methods having promise of being better than those commonly in use. In late years, I made special effort to try out modern designs of "stop-loss" traps and to improve methods of setting traps so as to drown captured animals with greater promptness and certainty.

All together, my personal experience in muskrat trapping during the months of commercially salable pelts has been in the taking of about 2,200 of the animals—fewer admittedly, than some trappers catch in single fur seasons. My trapping was done, however, under a fairly wide range of field conditions and now has as background over 40 years of association with veteran trappers of central North America as well as a general knowledge of the North American and European literature on muskrat trapping.

*   *   *

This book is an outgrowth of many years of cooperation with certain public agencies charged with administration of fur resources: the Iowa State Conservation Commission, the United States Fish and Wildlife Service, and the Game and Fisheries Branch of the Province of Manitoba. The

Hudson's Bay Company and the Wildlife Management Institute have also given the most excellent cooperation.

As concerns individuals, I owe thanks to more people than could possibly be mentioned by name: Iowa farm boys, Indians of northern wildernesses, European biologists, American refuge managers, game wardens, fur buyers, and humanitarians. The persons to whom I should express particular appreciation include Verl ("Jack") Black of Fort Dodge and Barnum, Iowa, with whom I trapped on a number of occasions; Dr. E. L. Kozicky, formerly of the Iowa Cooperative Wildlife Research Unit; Harold Mathiak of the Wisconsin Conservation Department; D. E. Denmark of the Hudson's Bay Company; and G. W. Malaher of the Government of Manitoba.

*　　*　　*

The selected references following the last chapter are intended to help the reader who may wish to study certain subjects in more detail, to get closer to source material than he could through reading this book. My reference list covers only a very small part of the literature that could be cited, but it is intentionally kept short to avoid unwieldiness.

*　　*　　*

It may be asked, in view of the countless articles, leaflets, bulletins, and some books that are already devoted to furbearers, including muskrats, just why more needs to be written? Of course, that is the sort of question for which any author should be prepared, whether he can answer it or not.

Let me say that I hope that this book may be informative and useful, that it may add to the perspective of its readers in a desirable way, and that it may be influential in reducing abuses and waste in the harvesting of especially muskrats for fur.

CONTENTS

CHAPTER I

Introduction

$\mathbf{A}$S A PRINCIPAL support of the fur trade, the musk-rat is one of the best-known mammals on earth. It is harvested by the millions each year. Insofar as it is not profitably bred and reared in captivity on a pelting basis, essentially all of the annual harvest of muskrat pelts comes from wild populations, even on the fenced-in marshes of the so-called "rat ranches."

Not all species of fur-bearing animals hold up well under human exploitation. Some species have thus been greatly reduced in range and numbers, but these are mainly unadaptable or slow-breeding forms, the pelts of which are, for some reason, commercial favorites. Effects of the fur trade upon population levels of fur-bearers depend not only upon the species of fur-bearer but also upon when, where, and under what conditions it lives and upon what harvesting methods are used and when, where, and under what conditions. Furthermore, our efforts to generalize are complicated by women's fashions, by engineering projects, by changes in land use, and by great changes in wild populations having no apparent connection with man.

Whatever may be the impacts of the fur trade on species that cannot "take it," the fur trade is not exterminating our North American muskrats. Overharvesting of muskrats can occur as when high fur prices promote "gleaning" or when the animals are vulnerably concentrated during drought years. When overharvesting does occur, legal protection for a single fur season usually restores a muskrat population—if conditions are otherwise favorable.

1

The muskrat is not adapted to stock-piling as a live fur resource. Years of study by Daniel Lay and Ted O'Neil on the famous muskrat marshes of the Gulf Coast brought out the great importance of one kind of bulrush (the Olney bulrush) to the muskrat populations of that region. "Eat-outs" of this bulrush by top-heavy muskrat populations can be so ruinous to muskrat environment that one of the biggest problems in maintaining the muskrat industry of those coastal marshes is to insure *adequate* muskrat harvesting during the fur season. The late H. L. Dozier and his colleagues came to much the same conclusion from many years of work on the marshes of the Atlantic Coast.

Muskrat populations of the northern states and northward are not nearly so likely to destroy their habitats through overuse. They have shown greater *self-limiting* tendencies. They are also subject to what can be among the deadliest of epidemic diseases.

The consequences to be expected from overharvesting of the muskrat for fur—even from chronic year-after-year overharvesting—are decreased fur yields during the trapping season rather than extermination. The distinction should be introduced here (before explaining more fully farther on in this book) that *moderately low* numbers of muskrats living in good environment enjoy many biological advantages, not the least of which is a greater relative peace and security during the breeding months. *Up to the point of overharvesting,* the more heavily muskrat populations are harvested for fur, the more young may be raised per female for the breeding stock remaining. This sort of natural compensating is common among the more prolific of wild species. But, at *very low* population levels, the muskrats may be so scarce and so scattered as to make mating less certain for what potential breeders are present in a locality.

*   *   *

To many thoughtful people, the principal question about harvesting wild fur-bearers is: "How humane and otherwise ethical are the harvesting methods?"

While some wild fur animals are harvested under some conditions by shooting or by other comparatively humane methods, a great many are taken by means of leg-grabbing steel traps. Personal attitudes toward capturing wild animals in steel traps vary from callousness or even sadism to the greatest pity or indignation—at times, even in the same person, depending upon what is being trapped, whether the victim is liked or disliked.

About the most that we are entitled to conclude as to how a trapped fur-bearer feels is that to be held alive in a steel trap must be painful. No one should assume that the sufferings of a non-human animal would be wholly comparable to what human sufferings might be, for, after all, much of man's capability for suffering results from his specialized nervous system and his imaginative powers. The skunk that phlegmatically ignores the stings of a swarm of bees (or of hornets!) when going after food that it wants must be much less sensitive to pain than is man, and the special readiness with which it may amputate a trapped foot seems further to confirm this thought. In contrast, members of the dog family probably are capable of much suffering when trapped. It is possible that some non-human forms know more acute physical pain than man does.

I suppose that I have seen examples of nearly everything that is likely to happen to the living flesh of north-central fur-bearers in steel traps. (I have also seen more than a little of the unpleasant ways in which wild creatures die "natural" deaths.) I could provide details as to what *can* happen to the *unluckiest* of trap victims (or to the *unluckiest* of their kinds suffering from fight wounds, disease, or old age) that would sicken many readers, but I do not see that such needs to be done. This book is intended to be constructive in outlook, with a scope including improvement of trapping methods; and it should here be sufficient to say of the worst of trapping methods that they need improvement.

As long as I can remember, I have read of ingenious efforts to devise humane traps. For specific purposes, such as capturing animals uninjured for marking or other scientific studies, or for stocking, breeding, or public exhibits, some of these humane traps are satisfactory. Most are built on the principle of a comfortable cage, and experts in their use may catch raccoons, skunks, minks, muskrats, and beavers, among the common North American fur-bearers. However, the leg-grabbing steel traps are generally much cheaper, lighter, more compact, more easily set or concealed, more familiar to trappers, and more adapted for taking fur-bearers on a commercial scale than are the humane traps so far to be seen on the public market.

A national organization offers a reward of $10,000.00 "for a humane trap that will be acceptable to commercial trappers as a substitute for existing steel-jawed traps." I hope that something really good emerges as a winner for this reward, but I confess that I do not know what it might be. My own thoughts about the possibility of an ideal trap have been attended by a complete lack of encouraging inspirations.

Human inventiveness already has been shown again and again in designs of steel traps put on the market during the first half of the Twentieth Century. Among these are traps intended to be quick killers or to seize an animal's leg or body in ways to prevent escape. Some appear to be, if anything, less humane than ordinary steel traps. Others may or may not be humane, depending upon how the victim gets into them. Others are merely steel traps with modernized features.

All of these traps, too, must pass their final critics, the

trappers. A trapper's verdict of "no good" has as much validity when applied to a new design of steel trap as to any other.

I believe that, for the present and the foreseeable future, our best hope of taking cruelty out of fur trapping is to work for more humane methods of using the traps that are accepted by the trappers. Substantial progress should be possible in this respect. Then, when and if humane traps that are practical for fur-trapping are ultimately invented and produced, they should still be in competitive positions on their own merits.

Drowning is the "key" to efficient and humane trapping of muskrats for fur with the traps that are in regular use among trappers. The methods of muskrat trapping to be described and advocated in this book will be, accordingly, drown-sets or those having good possibilities for drowning.

Not all traps set to drown may be expected to give a perfect record of success, for now and then an animal finds something to bear up its weight or manages to keep alive in some other way. A grown muskrat has the ability to remain submerged some 10 to 20 minutes if it quietly conserves its oxygen supply. Even when struggling under water and using up its oxygen (including oxygen "borrowed" from its body tissues) at a far more rapid rate, it may retain consciousness for several minutes. One should realistically keep in mind that an occasional muskrat mangles a trapped leg in a very short time despite promptness in drowning, but the drown-set still remains the answer to a great deal of what can be wrong in using steel traps for muskrat trapping.

For most muskrat trapping, my own choices of traps are those "stop-loss" designs available on the market since about 1950. The later designs of these traps are here specified, for some of the earlier had shortcomings to which trappers objected—though I never tried any that I did not consider superior to conventional steel traps.

The distinguishing feature of the "stop-loss" designs manufactured by American trap companies is a delayed-action metal guard that operates after closing of the trap jaws and holds the body of the animal away from the jaws in such a manner as to hinder twisting and escape. It is perfectly true that these "stop-losses" are steel traps and that an animal remaining conscious in one will suffer, but the "stop-lossess" offer exceptional opportunities for humane or nearly humane use. They are especially adapted to trapping in shallow water. In the course of our Iowa trapping experiments, muskrat after muskrat mercifully drowned in "stop-losses" in water only a few inches in depth over drought-exposed marsh bottoms, where trapping with ordinary steel traps could not have been done either humanely or without a high percentage of loss. The encumbering action of "stop-losses" greatly diminishes the chance of even a very large and strong muskrat swimming on the surface for any considerable time before drowning. A muskrat may also be stunned by the blow from the "stop-loss" guard.

(Harvesting of fur-animals other than muskrats is not only chiefly outside of the intended scope of this book but also has problems for which no comforting solutions are in sight. Next to the drown-sets that work so well for muskrats—but, unfortunately, for only a few other fur-bearers—sets made in places where their catches stand a good chance of quickly dying from cold are among the most merciful in their operation. I have so often observed wild creatures in various stages of freezing that I am convinced that death from cold is one of the easier ways of dying. Temperatures getting down to 20 to 40 degrees below zero Fahrenheit automatically bring relief from suffering for animals caught at exposed trap sites. In connection with cold-weather trapping in South Dakota and northern Minnesota, I usually found evidences of small fur-bearers dying in the early part of the night, and it plainly did not take long to freeze the trapped feet of animals as large as coyotes. Hence, the long traplines of northern wildernesses—requiring up to a couple of weeks to cover in some instances—do not always mean prolonged suffering for trap victims. But from my own experience, I would say that few are the circumstances justifying long intervals between trapline "runs" in north-central United States, and routine "runs" on all mornings that traps are set should almost always be feasible. The latter would not eliminate all of the abuses of overextended traplines or the basic faults of the steel trap but would help to do so.)

The respectability of a trapper's fur-harvesting is greatly conditioned by his attitude and skill. It is true that anyone using steel traps, snares, or even "humane" designs of traps may now and then have something go wrong that can not be prevented; but a tremendous amount of difference shows up in the performance of individual trappers.

*   *   *

Some aspects of the ways of life of muskrats are to be learned well in connection with trapping. Old-timers, who trap in great muskrat marshes for weeks or months each year and whose catches exceed a hundred a day under favorable trapping conditions, certainly learn something about muskrats in so doing; but it takes careful biological studies to go deeper. No one person—trapper, biologist, or lay observer—has any monopoly on the truth in such matters or knows or ever will know all that there is to know about the muskrat or about any other animal.

Biological studies of the muskrat have been carried on over the past three decades in almost all parts of the world where the species lives. The year-around campaigns of the British, French, Germans, and Dutch against the muskrat as an introduced pest have yielded information on its biology, and the Finns have been studying it for years as an addition to their fur resources. In North America, the species has been or is being studied from California north past the Arctic Circle, from the coastal marshes of the Gulf of Mexico north through north-central United States and central Canada, from the Atlantic coastal marshes northward into eastern Canada.

These studies represent much field work on the part of hundreds of different people—wading and poling and chopping ice and walking through thick vegetation. I have spent nearly 32,000 hours actually working on marshes and streams during the Iowa program of muskrat investigations, 1934-57; and there have been the examinations of thousands upon thousands of specimens and the laboratory experiments and the discussions of evidence and the reading and writing that the "scientific method" calls for in approaching complicated problems of living things.

The "scientific method" is in reality a combination of methods varying with the problems and with the people working on them. It is (or should be) just one thing: following the truth on the basis of the available evidence.

Despite the histories of some scientific discoveries made through happy accidents, one may hardly count on finding out much about muskrats by accidents. I, too, have had accidents, but mine were usually getting into mud over boot tops, falling out of a canoe, or having a finger bitten, and these were usually unaccompanied by flashes of insight into any matters that I did not already know about. Neither are illuminating and puncture-proof "theories" likely to descend upon the earnest student of our muskrats in his sleep, nor to emerge from mysterious formulas, to wipe away vexatious questions.

In the scientific work about which I feel competent to write, the distinctions between the possible and the impossible may not be at all clear. One's approaches to a big problem must be directed toward questions about which something definite is to be learned, such as sex and age ratios of the muskrats, sizes and numbers of litters, mortality, food habits, responses to emergencies, population changes from year to year. Animals may be marked in order to make them individually recognizable, or breeding territories and disease "hotspots" may be plotted on maps. Thus, we try to lay a solid foundation of facts, at the same time looking for the more promising leads in exploring the more elusive unknowns.

The "scientific method" implies work over sufficient periods of time and under a sufficient variety of conditions to become meaningful. A lot of the work may be drudgery, and some of it may be messy or uncomfortable or perhaps even dangerous. Imagination has its place in wildlife research if tempered by reality, whether in planning a project, in carrying on the work, or in appraising results when results exist to be appraised; but the "scientific method" does not—or should not—consist of straining to prove the preconceived idea, the pet "theory." It consists—or should consist—of searching for the pertinent facts, getting them down on paper, then studying them from different angles for guidance in arriving at conclusions. Conclusions should always be regarded as subject to review and modification whenever such may be called for by newer or better evidence.

In the more difficult of biological investigations, there are no substitutes for adequate numbers of observations or samples—not just a few of the sorts that one might pick up incidental to being in the out-of-doors but rather hundreds or thousands of observations or samples recorded systematically, day after day, and year after year. There are no substitutes for records permanently down on paper, no substitutes for notes written at the times of the events observed.

*　　*　　*

The following chapters concerning muskrats fall broadly into two sections, one on biology and the other on management and harvesting. Neither section is claimed to be a complete and final treatment. Each is written with certain objectives in mind.

The biological chapters are intended to introduce the reader to information that he might care to have about muskrats living like muskrats, about muskrats being themselves in their own ways. The management and harvesting chapters do not attempt to cover every known method of managing and harvesting muskrats—only the methods that I regard as the best among those of which I know.

CHAPTER II

About Muskrats and Their Way of Life

IN SKELETON and body build, the muskrat is like an overgrown meadow mouse, but its flattened swimming tail and partly webbed hind feet make it more adapted than the meadow mouse for an aquatic life. It is a native of North America, occurring naturally in a large proportion of those marshes, lakes, and streams of the continent having suitable environment for it. Sixteen more or less closely related living forms of muskrats are listed in a recent publication by Gerrit S. Miller, Jr., and Remington Kellogg of the U. S. National Museum, and a half dozen extinct forms have been described from fossil beds dating back to Ice-Age times.

The form known as the Common or Eastern Muskrat not only occupies muskrat habitats over most of the eastern half of the United States and adjacent Canada but it also seems to be the one that has so thoroughly colonized much of the Old World after having been introduced there by man, mostly during the first quarter of the present century. Its distribution in the wetlands of northern and central Eurasia now seems to be almost general, except for a few places remaining isolated from its areas of abundance on the mainland.

The Louisiana Muskrat may at times outnumber the Common Muskrat in North America, but its geographic range is small in terms of square miles—consisting of the coastal marshes from southeastern Texas to southwestern Alabama and centering in southern Louisiana. The Maryland or Virginia Muskrat is another coastal marsh form that can be abundant locally, with a range extending southward from New Jersey and Delaware to North Carolina.

The Rocky Mountain Muskrat, the Great Plains Muskrat, the Northwestern Muskrat, and the Hudson Bay Muskrat are all forms with large ranges that are passably well indicated by the common names of the respective muskrats. (The Rocky Mountain Muskrat does occur in many places other than in the mountains, and the Hudson Bay Muskrat is far more an animal of an extensive region west of Hudson Bay rather than one having its distribution centered about the Bay, itself.) There are also an Alaska Peninsula Muskrat, a Labrador Muskrat, a Newfoundland Muskrat, an Oregon Coast Muskrat, and a Nevada Muskrat, likewise named on the basis of geography.

In our American Southwest, we have four forms having restricted ranges. One—the Pecos River Muskrat—seems well on the way to be squeezed out of existence by man's engineering, which has resulted in the diversion of water from its environment for irrigation purposes. The Colorado River Muskrat, once confined to the lower Colorado River Valley, got the opposite "break" from man's engineering activities: After the reclamation of the Imperial Valley area of southeastern California through diversion of water from the Colorado River, this form of muskrat found itself in a position to expand its range, often into places where it was not wanted. This is the only muskrat of which I know that is positively reported from Mexico, where it occurs in a small area. The other two living forms in North America are one in the Gila River and tributaries of southern and central Arizona and southwestern New Mexico and one in the Virgin River Valley of southwestern Utah. The Southwest has also been the scene of venturesome artificial stocking of muskrats from different sources.

These 16 recognized forms of muskrats differ or resemble one another in size, coloration, and pelt value. They are all muskrats, despite their hereditary differences and the impacts of differing environments upon them, all living for the most part as muskrats can be expected to live anywhere that muskrats can live. If any North American region that I have seen lacks muskrats, the reasons are usually apparent to people who know muskrats and what muskrats need for year-around environment.

The southeastern region of the United States gives us a baffling exception. No proposed explanations seem wholly to account for the thinning out and disappearance of muskrats in Alabama and Georgia as the Florida boundary is approached. The ranges of three forms—the Louisiana, Common, and Maryland Muskrats—reach for the vast Florida wetlands but they do not get there. The little so-called round-tailed muskrat living in the Okefinokee swamp and southward into Florida is *not* a real muskrat. Nor is it likely that real muskrats very often get within a radius of 200 miles of the round-tail's range, even along streams that have muskrats in their headwaters.

Some differences, however, may be seen in what muskrats do and in how they live. Freezing weather is infrequent on the Louisiana marshes, and muskrats there are said to drown under the ice when waters are sealed over. In the Far North and at high altitudes in the West, muskrats spend a nine-month winter under several feet of ice. The Rocky Mountain Muskrat lives in a variety of habitats, from typical valley marshes and streams to beaver pools at 10,000 feet, beaches along the Pacific Ocean, desert springs, irrigation ditches and reservoirs, and in almost every thinkable combination of food and water furnishing living requirements for muskrats. The Common Muskrat has subarctic living conditions at one end of its range, about James Bay. At the other end of its range, in Louisiana and Mississippi, it occurs close enough to the Gulf of Mexico to inter-breed with the Louisiana Muskrat. Between James Bay and the Gulf, the Common Muskrat lives in Iron Range and Ozark and Appalachian and corn belt streams, in the bayous of great rivers, in ditch pools, tile flows, farm ponds, along the shores of open water lakes, and in the reeds and rushes and cattails of glacial marshes. The Great Plains Muskrat lives in the Sand Hill marshes of Nebraska, in glacial marshes in the Dakotas, in some streams of the eastern Rockies, in streams of the Badlands and gumbo plains, and in artificial impoundments of the "West River Country," from Texas and Oklahoma up to southern Saskatchewan and Manitoba. Northward, the main strongholds of the Northwestern Muskrat and the Hudson Bay Muskrat are in the marshes of inland river deltas—in the many millions of acres of the Saskatchewan, Peace, and Athabaska river deltas, and, still farther northward toward and past the Arctic Circle, in the delta of the Mackenzie River.

Wherever they live, muskrats sit out flood waters in about the same way, whether they take refuge on beaches, levee banks, hay stacks, floating logs, tree limbs, or ice cakes. During droughts, they deepen their passage channels in about the same way and repair their burrows or lodges with wads of vegetation, mud, stones, sticks, corn cobs, mollusk shells, and old bones, with what they can find and move. They are not too proud to try to live in polluted water or under a water tank in a farm yard if they must, nor to construct a lodge in a low-lying corn field out of dirt and stalks if that is the best that they can do under the circumstances. They have a strong will to live and a way of keeping at their job of staying alive as long as they have anything to do it with. If they do not actually inherit the earth, it is not because they are unwilling to try.   *   *   *

The basic living requirements for muskrats anywhere are the right kinds of food and enough of it and neither too much nor too little fresh or brackish water. If muskrats try to live either in a place rich in food and a little short of water, or in one with plenty of water but short of food, they generally make out better in the place with the abundance of food—though they still must have a minimum of water that neither freezes nor dries up.

High-quality food is especially important for northern muskrats during the cold weather months. In Iowa, the food of foods for stream-dwelling muskrats is that state's famous ear corn, which is sometimes stored by the bushel in the tunnels and chambers and blind alleys of the larger burrow systems. Marsh-dwelling populations of muskrats on the Iowa study areas seldom raid cornfields as long as "natural" foods are available to them. Their outstanding "natural" foods are rootstocks and other nutritious parts of cattails, bulrushes, and arrowheads (duck potatoes). As a rule, the marsh muskrats go after food whenever they need it, summer or winter, and do their mealtime foraging within 50 or 100 yards of their home lodges or burrows.

Few types of food are really stored by our north-central muskrats, and storage habits are by no means of uniform occurrence. It often happens that the material from which lodges are built consists of the nutritious rootstocks as well as the coarse stems of especially those bulrushes known as "three-square." If the muskrats become hungry, they may ultimately eat these rootstocks as they find them imbedded in the sides and tops of the lodges. Other material that was originally carried to a lodge or burrow for bedding or construction may likewise be eaten by the muskrats, but such should not be confused with purposefully stored food. Other than ear corn, about the only food likely to be stored by Iowa muskrats is the bulb of several kinds of arrowhead (duck potato), which may be systematically packed in both burrows and lodges of certain sloughs having large quantities available to the muskrats.

During my own studies, I looked for years without finding evidence of marsh muskrats storing duck potatoes (or anything else), then began finding more and more storing on certain marshes or parts of marshes. As it looks to me now, a small group of muskrats begins storing, and then increasing numbers of the animals imitate this behavior until a whole population may be doing it wherever the duck potatoes grow. This is more of an activity of muskrats living in drought-threatened shallows, and mud-plastered dry lodges may be notable repositories for stored bulbs. When the "tradition" becomes established in a population, storage chambers of deep-water lodges of rushy construction may also be filled with bulbs, sometimes a peck or more of them in a single chamber. Neighboring populations living under comparable circumstances may or may not store.

My conclusion is that such storage habits are repeatedly lost and regained by muskrat populations. If food and water conditions are so favorable that the muskrats can find all they need to eat at all times simply by going after it, their incentives for storage are slight. In a year or two, the individuals that practice storage are replaced by those that do not. If conditions again become such as to promote storage tendencies, some individuals of new generations may reestablish the old patterns—and there they are, digging, carrying, packing, walling off, as if they knew exactly what to do.

Muskrats should not be regarded as imaginative or intellectual or capable of much planning ahead, but they do show a fair amount of something like common-sense practicality in their daily lives. They are entirely capable of learning to adjust in simple ways that are advantageous to them.

Muskrats of the north-central region seldom experience a food crisis during the growing season for plant life, except occasionally through flood or drought emergencies. They may prefer certain foods in spring and summer when they can get them, and the case histories from our study areas indicate that muskrat populations feeding on young corn plants or cattails or a few other of the choicer foods live with less fighting and raise bigger and healthier families than those having only the coarser grasses, or weeds or brush, for their warm-weather foods. However, differences in nutritive values of summer foods do not have the importance for muskrats as may differences in winter foods. A wide variety of marsh or stream-edge vegetation meets their dietary needs passably well until the weather turns cold.

Some muskrats behave like congenital vegetarians; others show the "meat tooth." On the same tract of marsh at the same time, some muskrats eat dead or dying fishes or the bodies of dead or helpless young water birds or young muskrats, while other muskrats ignore this sort of material. There is nothing like an excellent source of plant food to make vegetarians out of muskrats. Whenever flesh-feeding by the muskrats occurs on a large scale in a north-central area, it is strong evidence that the animals are short of plant foods. Furthermore, I have never seen specimens from muskrat populations living on high protein diets that were in fat condition, though I have not always been sure whether that resulted from their high protein diets or simply from their not having enough of anything to eat.

Wintering muskrats of the north-central region leave

heaps of fresh water clam shells about icy feeding places as symptoms of "hard times," along with fish remains and odd bits of vegetation and the inedible or poisonous egg masses of frogs. This feeding debris is seen early in the winter at holes in the ice along streams or lake shores, and, as winter progresses, similar remains are left in tunnels and nests in snowdrifts near passageways to the water. Sluggish mud turtles have tails and feet gnawed away from the edges of their shells, and the muskrats even open up the shells to eat of the soft parts within.

In ice-sealed waters where fishes are winter-killing from lack of oxygen, many of the last living fishes—bullheads, conspicuously—crowd into the water of the channels and plunge holes of the muskrat lodges and burrows, to gulp air and work hard at staying alive. Some flip out of the water and lie on the beds in the lodge chambers; others become partly frozen into the surrounding ice while still alive; and, finally, there may be fishes nearly everywhere inside of the muskrat retreats or encased in the ice.

Although I have seen these squirming masses of fishes or their floating bodies left quite untouched by fat muskrats feeding on lush stands of cattails and bulrushes, the muskrats of marshes having the thinner stands of cattails, bulrushes, and other choice plant foods may take bullhead flesh along with the plant food. One collection of 66 muskrat stomachs from a population wintering under such conditions contained bullheads in 27, and the volume of flesh food exceeded the volume of plant food. This flesh-feeding did not imply any real desperation on the part of the muskrats. It served merely to supplement their otherwise rather skimpy diet of first-class plant food.

Under some conditions, muskrat diets resemble those of local minks—animals that are as strictly carnivorous in the wild as any that I can think of. Sometimes, the minks industriously drag out and pack frogs and fishes by the hundreds in snowdrift tunnels over water holes or leave them stacked in frozen piles on the landings. The muskrats gnaw on the meaty tails of the mink-piled fishes as they would on their own plunder.

(Such close association between muskrats and their ancient enemies, the minks, does not necessarily result in severe predation being suffered by the muskrats. As long as the muskrats are in possession of their normal faculties for defense or escape, and as long as the environment is in their favor, they rarely have to let themselves be caught by minks. The many years of studies of relationships between minks and muskrats on Iowa fur areas brought out that about 70% of the feeding by minks upon muskrats represented only scavenging in response to dying of muskrats from causes other than predation. Disease proved to be almost always at the bottom of this non-predacious mortality of muskrats that the minks were so ready to exploit. The other 30% of the feeding of minks upon muskrat flesh, which actually did represent predation upon the muskrats, occurred mostly because muskrats were in exceptional difficulties either with other muskrats or with their living conditions. More about this is reserved for later chapters.)

*   *   *

Like top-quality foods, water—in the right quantities and places—is of more clear importance in the lives of northern muskrats in winter than in summer. Short of the ruinous stages of droughts, muskrats *may* get along during the warmer months with surprisingly little water, perhaps with no more than wet mud in the channels leading to the entrances of their lodges and burrows. One sees packed trails leading from the burrows of a nearly-dry ditch to a cornfield or apple orchard. On a marsh, trails lead from exposed lodges into clumps of cattails or bulrushes. Or, there may be other evidences of regular activities on land. Often, under these conditions, the musk-rats obviously maintain themselves with little or no loss from the general run of their predatory enemies. Yet, a water shortage can be a most serious handicap to muskrat populations even during periods of comfortable weather—especially if the larger predatory mammals dig into lodges or ground retreats after live muskrats.

Such enterprise on the part of the predators may not show up at all in an area or, over a period of years, it may become of wide occurrence. There is reason to think that large-scale digging into dry or shallow-water muskrat lodges by pigs, raccoons, and members of the dog family usually starts as a result of these animals smelling dead muskrats within, particularly during die-offs from disease. After local digging traditions become established, it may be hard to distinguish between the summer-time search for mere carrion and the search for helpless sizes of young musk-rats and other catchable individuals.

In severe winter weather, what determines a critical lack of water depends both upon the behavior of the musk-rats and the circumstances under which they live.

A group of muskrats sitting out the winter in a burrow full of ear corn or arrowhead bulbs may come through splendidly in a place that, from the outside, looks dry and uninhabited. One well-isolated, dried-out pond in the midst of an Iowa cornfield had no external evidence of living muskrats during early winter—though muskrats had been very busy in the corn, wearing trails between their burrows and the cornfield, before the ground froze. I recall the abandoned-looking burrow entrances and the gradual bleaching and drying of the old fall "sign" as the weeks passed. Then, when a midwinter rain refilled the pond, and clear ice formed over the newly collected water, muskrats swam back and forth beneath the ice, going in and out of the same burrow entrances that had seemed so lifeless a few days before.

Although complete exposure of a marsh bottom to freezing air temperatures may mean more hardship and danger than muskrats seeking cattail and bulrush rootstocks can endure week after week even at Iowa latitudes, only a little water over the bases of the cattails and bulrushes at freeze-up may at times assure resident muskrats of some access to good food. Perhaps three to six inches of water over the bottom of one of our cattail or bulrush marshes makes the difference between most or none of the local animals getting through. Water a foot to a foot-and-a-half deep over these food-rich bottoms may provide good to excellent wintering conditions for Iowa muskrats and also for muskrats living much farther north if the ice is covered by insulating snow. Large snowdrifts make parts of some dry marshes habitable for muskrats to some degree if the drifts form (and persist) before the bottom freezes deeply. Cattail and reed growths are especially good snow-catchers.

The same depths of water that would mean comfort and safety to muskrats wintering in a cattail or bulrush marsh may be wholly inadequate for muskrats depending upon a food supply of coontail, pondweeds, and other submerged plant life to be found *only* in the water lying above the bottom of a marsh or slough. Central Iowa muskrats living in such waters may get along well until about the first of February, only to find themselves in a desperate situation almost suddenly, as the last of their floating food becomes encased in ice. Some animals stall off the crisis for a few days—or longer, if the weather moderates—by eating the interiors of their lodges, eating what waterlily roots they can still reach by deepening and extending channels in the still-unfrozen mud bottom, eating the bullheads and minnows in the last wet passageways, gnawing through ice and frozen mud to reach trifling sources of nourishment when they can find it.

The final stages of freeze-out crises follow so much of a pattern on central Iowa muskrat areas that one might almost set up a time-schedule. With encasement of their food supply and restriction of their movements under the ice, the muskrats start coming outside to see what they can do for themselves. This usually is not much. They walk on the ice from lodge to lodge or travel to shore. Their first journeys of this sort have the appearance of being more or less cautious round trips. As the desperation of the muskrats increases, so also do footloose movements. Some of the animals wander completely out of the area. Winter-wandering can be so deadly for muskrats in a cold climate that the individuals "staying put" in their familiar home ranges, freeze-out emergencies notwithstanding, have the better prospects for survival. When matters become bad enough, however, it makes scant difference in the end what the unlucky animals do.

Under such overwhelming handicaps, the muskrats are killed by opportunistic minks, either inside or outside of their dry and frozen lodges. They are killed by dogs, foxes, or large birds of prey while they wander. They are killed by motor traffic on highways. They die of wounds received in fighting among themselves. They weaken and die from disease. They freeze to death—out in the open, in improvised nests of weedy or rush growths, in holes under tree roots, in openings of pressure-buckled ice ridges—or almost anywhere, in their old home ranges or out of them.

The tips of the tails of muskrats freeze first when long exposed to cold. If that is the worst that happens, the animals gnaw away the frozen and festering tips and go through the rest of their lives with bobbed tails. In the more advanced cases of freezing, eyes and feet freeze, or the victims may be so beaten by cold that they just huddle and die. Where winters are long, cold, and short of snow, the descent of frost lines to depths of several feet can bring death to the majority of muskrats of tremendous areas.

Despite the sensitivity of the bare extremities of muskrats to cold air, the animals, at least from Iowa northwestward, have certain capabilities for manipulating freezing and frozen materials. As long as our north-central muskrats can obtain wet mud or wet vegetation for plugging openings in their retreats (mink holes, cracks, cave-ins, the holes that they themselves make in getting outside at times when forced by hunger to forage on the surface, etc.), they may do well in avoiding serious consequences from exposure to cold—always assuming that they continue getting enough to eat.

The view held by some trappers and naturalists that muskrats are actually imprisoned by frost is unsupported by any first-hand information that I have. Our Iowa evidence indicates that normal muskrats can and do gnaw out of frozen quarters whenever they wish if they have the time to do it. They may be drowned there or under unbroken ice by entrapping flood waters before they can save themselves; they may starve in a frozen lodge or succumb to cold or wounds or disease; but I do not see how mere ice can long imprison our northern muskrats in their living quarters if they are strong enough to make a real effort to get out.

Muskrats, however, do not seem to have anywhere nearly the ability to get into a frozen lodge or burrow as they have ability to get out of one, nor to gnaw downward through ice as to gnaw upward. At the same times when some may be wandering hopelessly over the ice outside of lodges, others begin the rehabilitation of frozen lodges by gnawing away, from below, the ice-seals over plunge holes. They may gnaw upwards through a foot or more of ice covering the deeper water of a slough or at some spot on the lake ice 50 to 100 yards out from the burrows of the shore. This may be done with bodies completely submerged, and the first sign of such activity may be a muskrat sitting beside a small hole out on the ice, amid wet ice splinters and perhaps some heaped coontail. Next, a chimney-like nest or a little covered feed house appears, with a muskrat in it that, presumably, feels as if it had done something.

Flooding during severe winter weather can subject muskrats to a rather special type of emergency. The most deadly flood that I ever saw turned the bottomlands of a central Iowa creek into a steaming lake at an air temperature of nearly 30 degrees below zero Fahrenheit. The muskrats of the creek were forced to take refuge wherever they could in open fields and in ice jams, and the resulting mortality was complete for some miles along the creek channel and the flooded borders of the valley. More frequent and less deadly are the melt waters from thaws that now and then fill up the air spaces beneath the ice of a marsh or slough.

In places where plant material, muskrat lodges, or uneven topography of a marsh bottom hold the ice suspended as water recedes in the course of a winter, muskrats may withdraw from their accustomed living chambers in the lodges and make adjustments under the ice. They build nests between layers of ice or in the networks of channels and paths over which they travel, often considerable distances from the chambers used while the water remained up to the bottom of the surface ice. The upper parts of

FIGURE 1. "Wherever they live, muskrats sit out flood waters, in about the same way." Photo by Jim Sherman, Iowa State Conservation Commission.

FIGURE 2. Muskrats building a lodge on a Canadian marsh. Photo by D. E. Denmark, Hudson's Bay Company.

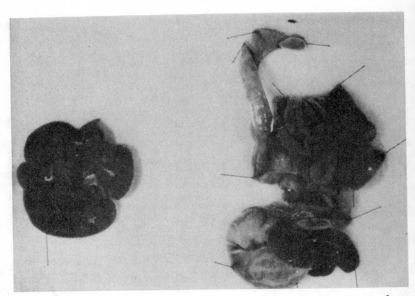

FIGURE 3. Common types of the hemorrhagic disease of muskrats may show, in addition to intestinal hemorrhages (upper right), liver spots (left) resembling those of tularemia. Photo by Iowa State College Photoservice.

FIGURE 4. One of the "increasingly dissatisfied . . . animals that keep popping out of the ice every time that a late-winter thaw encourages them to do so . . ." Photo by Jim Sherman, Iowa State Conservation Commission.

the lodges may, at such times, be left unrepaired by the muskrats if opened by minks or other animals from the outside, yet this in itself is no indication that the muskrats are confronted by a crisis. It is when water from above pours into the muskrat-occupied places below the ice that the muskrats must return to their old retreats or otherwise adjust to the new changes. When, as undeniably can happen in our North American interior, a thaw putting down melt water is followed immediately by freezing cold, muskrats may have to work fast and sometimes in exposed positions to do their necessary repairing. There may be a day or two of tail-freezing, mink predation, and social upsets and frictions among the muskrats before they live safely and comfortably again.

Some muskrats thus forced by melt waters to leave their quarters start cross-country movements, particularly in late winter or early spring as the breeding season of muskrats comes on. They may or may not live through it, depending upon whether spring is, in truth, "just around the corner" or whether more is to come of subzero temperatures that kill exposed muskrats irrespective of calendar dates.   *   *   *

Movements of muskrats have been studied in many parts of North America, both through marking of individuals and through field observations at times of population adjustments.

At one extreme, we get records of marked individuals being taken months or a year or so later at sites a mile, or three miles, or over 20 miles from their birth places. Occasionally, an observer is lucky enough to be on the scene or to be in an exceptionally good position to "read sign" when large-scale movements of muskrats are in progress. The latter sometimes mean almost total depopulation of some tracts of wetlands or massing of muskrats elsewhere. We may have practically all of the muskrats of mile after mile of a watercourse moving either upstream or downstream during late summer or early fall, and, in the following spring, repopulation by as many breeding adults moving in as the watercourse had the spring before. We have proven cases of from 100 to 300 muskrats pouring into a local area to establish residence there in late summer or fall. In one case, about 140 came into an attractive but virtually muskrat-less marsh during about the first week of October.

Yet, free-living muskrats do spend their entire lives, from birth through middle age and possibly through old age (which means up to the age of three or four years), in restricted areas. On our Iowa marshes, animals marked with numbered metal tags while very young were commonly recovered at ages of several months to one-and-one-half years at or near (as within 200 yards of) their birthplaces. "Home-body" muskrats include those of any age and of either sex, and theirs is the normal behavior of muskrats living under conditions promoting contentment.

Muskrat home ranges overlap in a variable manner but they comprise the areas in which individuals know their way around and in which they feel (so far as we humans are entitled to judge) that they belong. Trespassers on home ranges are likely to get into trouble chiefly if they are strangers or if they come around at times when the established residents are disinclined to be charitable.

A particular subdivision of the home range, toward which the individual may feel much more possessive, is called a territory, to be defended against trespassing whenever occasion for defense arises. A female suckling a litter of young is the muskrat that usually shows territoriality in its more acute form, and its defensive activities center about the lodge or burrow system containing the young.

In discussing the subject of territorial behavior in muskrats, we should keep in mind that the term is man-made and that the muskrats are under no compulsion to make their behavior conform to human definitions. One muskrat is so touchy that, wherever it goes, it can be seen attacking other muskrats that come near it. Some mother muskrats kill their own newly weaned young in driving them away from nests before a new litter is to be born or attack any other muskrat even approaching the vicinity of nests containing their young. Another suckling mother allows the progeny from the two or three earlier litters of her season's breeding to stay around without hindrance or allows mixed adults and young from neighboring groups to enter at will the chambers containing her own family. Rarely, two females simultaneouly keep their own suckling litters in the same lodge or in the same chamber—though, in general, the females maintain their territorial headquarters 20 to 50 yards or farther apart.

In general, also, the adult females seem less tolerant of crowding than adult males during the breeding months, despite the fact that the males are the more conspicuously bitten from fighting. Our evidence from Iowa marshes suggests that males may not be more quarrelsome, only more likely to be on the receiving end when biting becomes savage. One summer, toward the end of the active breeding season on an overpopulated marsh, young of different ages were to be seen heaping themselves about patient-looking adults on open-air sitting places. Several of these obviously tolerant adults were collected as scientific specimens from their respective assemblages of youngsters and they all proved to be males—this, over a large tract of marsh on which there had been much slaughtering of innocents by mother muskrats.

Doubtless, the responsiveness of many muskrats to the presence of others is partly conditioned by what the others do. Not much "turn-the-other-cheek" philosophy can be detected in the social relations of normal muskrats. Weaned young that attack with great viciousness other young that come near them (or eat the suckling young that they may find in nests) may not be more popular with their fellow muskrats than adults that slash recklessly wherever they go. Even naturally well-disposed muskrats should not be expected to encourage unpleasant visitors. And it should be expected that muskrat populations tend to show irritability when uncomfortable, discontended, or in a real crisis.

Habitual wanderers of late spring or early summer show the most signs of getting into trouble. Whether we call them social misfits or outcasts or plain tramps, whether they look for trouble or can not keep out of it, they are usually a battered lot. When they meet with a "property-owner" that does not want them around, they usually come out on the short end of fights. These unfortunates may be sick, aged, stunted, or merely young. They may look like normal animals except perhaps for their many wounds. They may be of either sex but mainly males, and mainly males for the reason that males ordinarily outnumber females and make up a larger proportion of the surplus adults often present early in the breeding season.

One of the prerogatives of any functional muskrat living in a state of freedom is to try to adjust to unsatisfactory conditions by moving. It shifts its main center of activity from 20 to 100 yards, or up to many miles, in response to food or water shortages, to disturbances by other animals (including other muskrats), or to the physiological changes of the breeding season. If adjustments are only from one part of a muskrat's range to another, or along a stream bed or marsh bottom in gradual and orderly stages, the behavior of the mover should be considered normal under the circumstances. Such an animal is still doing nothing rash nor committing itself to any course of action without a certain amount of testing as it goes, and, up to this point, behaves as if still "at home."

A good deal of the long-distance movement that now and then occurs along watercourses must also be considered normal, but the distinction should be kept in mind that the participants are taking chances in that they do not know what they are headed for. Nor, if they do find habitable environment at the other end of their journey, are they assured of being able to live there. The responses of muskrats in residence are as much of a part of new environment as the physical features. Sometimes mass migrations occur along definite routes away from overcrowded or deteriorating areas into areas in which no muskrats can long stay alive—as into the deserts surrounding some western marshes.

The most favorable time of year for north-central muskrats to change home ranges or otherwise make big adjustments involving other muskrats is in late summer and early fall. This is after the breeding-season jealousies have quieted down and before the threat of cold weather again reminds selfish muskrats of the realities of a limited and not unusually congenial world. Late summer and early fall can be a nice time of year (if it does not become too dry), with plenty to eat for the eaters, and with Nature being as mellow as she ever is. Enterprising youngsters then explore the outskirts of their parents' home ranges or work deeper into some of the home ranges of total strangers without necessarily risking attacks. In fact, one seldom finds a bite wound on any muskrats that are circulating in strange places at this time of year.

There always seem to be some exceptions: some cranky adults that do not like company, apparently ever, some

mean ones that apparently can not pass up an opportunity
to lay open a hip joint or get in a bite through a tail or
over a kidney if a stranger acts a little timid, some getting
too old or too sick to be companionable. Thus, no one
should conclude that all must be sweetness, light, and good
will between strange muskrats at this season, either. Yet,
for those muskrats that feel impelled to go out into the
world, in quest of greener pastures or greener marshes or
of only a puddle in which they can wet their feet, this is
the time to do it.

As distinguished from the orderly types of movements
in which muskrats may engage while retaining their full
faculties as muskrats—the more or less intelligent and
practical, making-the-best-of-what-they-have behavior—we
can have a frantic and footloose wandering over the
countryside, into towns and farm yards, into almost any
place that muskrats can reach but in which they do not
belong.

Let anyone who meets a muskrat on foot on dry land
watch out, or he may be bitten by an animal that has
equipment to bite with! The propensity of such land-
wandering muskrats to rear up and rush at one's legs,
teeth first, gives rise to many rabies scares. Muskrats are
susceptible to rabies, and a few cases of rabid muskrats
are on record, but the alleged unprovoked attacks by muskrats have ways of being provoked in the sense that any
living creature of formidable size that overtakes or con-
fronts a muskrat on land is recognized as a potential
enemy. Gentle old ladies, children, horses, cattle, even
rolling tumbleweeds, may be attacked by desperate muskrats acting as if they felt cornered. It is quite natural for
muskrats to act this way when surprised in places where
they have no chance to find water for refuge. No one need
impute to rabies the efforts of muskrats to take care of

themselves. Whatever else may be said of them, normal muskrats are not sissies, and, when scared in addition, they can be savage.

On our study areas, the numbers and proportions of the muskrats thus wandering away from watercourses as if they really were lost vary greatly from year to year. This sort of thing depends not only upon the numbers and proportions of animals having the common physical handicaps of sickness, old age, wounds, etc., or beset by the common types of emergencies, but also upon certain groupings of calendar years. The matter is so complex that it should discourage adherents of the "Nature-is-an-open-book" school of thought from assuming that what is in Nature's book is either more legible or self-explanatory than actually is the case.

The year-to-year histories of muskrat populations studied in central and northern Iowa show that the year-groups of 1936-37, 1945-47, and 1956-57 were those of unusual restlessness and intolerances. The opposites in behavior prevailed during the year-groups of 1941-43 and 1951-52. For the other years, the behavior of the muskrats in these respects tended to be in between the two extremes. What this meant on the Iowa marshes and streams was that the adult muskrats tolerated about three times as much crowding of territories during their breeding seasons in the 1941-43 and 1951-52 year-groups as in 1936-37, 1945-47, and 1956-57, and that the tendencies of the species to fight and wander were accordingly diminished in 1941-43 and 1951-52. The muskrats, young and old, also displayed far less inclination to "stay home" in the face of such emergencies as drought exposure during the 1936-37, 1945-47, and 1956-57 year-groups.

These particular differences in behavior do not seem to be associated with climatic differences or with anything

conveniently understandable. Living conditions in central
Iowa looked splendid in the late summer and early fall of
1946, yet a moderate population of muskrats engaged in
the most wholesale abandonment of habitats and cross-
country wandering shown by 24 years of records. At the
same time of year in 1952, the same central Iowa areas
had about twice as many muskrats as in 1946 and were
subject to a considerable period of drought, as well, yet
the amount of wandering taking place in 1952 was much
less than in 1946.

One of the most interesting aspects of these year-group-
ings is the extent to which they line up with the celebrated ups and downs of the snowshoe hares and ruffed
grouse of the "North Woods" part of our north-central
region. For the first half of the Twentieth Century, and
for this region, the years ending in or near the sixes and
sevens have been pretty much the "cyclic lows" for such
hares and grouse, and the years ending in or near the ones
and twos have been the "cyclic highs." Just why the wetland muskrats should be acting like malcontents when
forms of life of such dissimilar habits as hares and grouse
decline hundreds of miles away cannot be well explained
from present knowledge. It could be that some unknown
factor exerts, in a recurring pattern, a depressive influence
on a wide variety of unrelated animal life on at least a
regional scale. We may hope to know more about this
some day.

In this connection, it should be emphasized that numerical fluctuations of central Iowa muskrats have *not* been
in general agreement with the fluctuations of the hares
and grouse over the period of our studies. In Iowa, the
irregular and frequent occurrence of the droughts to
which muskrats are so vulnerable would in itself rule out
chances for much regularity in our muskrat fluctuations.

In considering the apparent line-ups between the fortunes of the hares and grouse on the one hand, and the muskrats on the other, we would get farther if we ignored the fluctuations of the muskrats and scrutinized instead the ways in which their lives did conform to the time schedule of the hares and grouse and the "10-year game cycle." We should consider not only the changes in behavior of the muskrats but changes in breeding performances and changes in resistance to disease, as well—and maybe other changes that no one has been looking for, as yet.

Nothing should be put forth as being more complicated than it is, but where muskrats live and how they do so, and why and why not, and the modifying "ifs," "ands," and "buts" cannot be expressed in a few simple words and still give anyone much accurate information. The complexities are not my invention. They came right out of Nature's book; but it can be said of Nature that she does not seem to be concerned about whether her book is open or closed, or whether what is in the book is arranged according to what humans consider proper order, or whether her readers arrive at correct answers at all. The responsibility for arriving at correct answers is strictly ours.

With this much understood about Nature and her book, let us see what else we can dig out and piece together about the muskrats.

CHAPTER III

More About Muskrats

At FIRST GLANCE, it might seem logical that, the more muskrats there are to breed, the more breeding will be done. Or that the more breeding that muskrats do, the more muskrats there will be. Or that the more muskrats we have this year, the more we may expect next year. We may reason that, if it is desirable to have 1,000 muskrats on a marsh, it is twice as desirable to have 2,000. We may reason that, if we know the average number of young muskrats born per litter and the average number of litters born per adult female or per breeding pair for a region during a year or a group of years, we can apply those figures to a given marsh at a given time and expect to come out right side up statistically. Or we may graduate into balance sheet mathematics full of "conservative estimates" sprinkled with a few facts that are assumed to "stay put," whether they do or not.

From here, it may be only a jump or two into fallacies that perhaps fall a bit short of those indulged in by the young lady in the story who had such ambitious plans for the unhatched chickens of a basket of eggs, yet which can be adequately misleading in their own ways.

In principle, there is nothing wrong with calculating from what we know and trying to get an idea of what may happen. But, as concerns muskrats, we may well be careful when tempted to put figures down on paper.

If so many young are born per female and there are so many females in an area . . . If so many of the young are killed by this enemy and so many more by that one, if so many drown, die of disease, wander away, are abandoned by parents, how many do we have left when the trapping season comes around? All so scientific and with so much common sense behind it—nothing wrong except that the essential facts that must be considered include those that seldom are.

Following are some of the conclusions drawn from almost a quarter-century of detailed records on Iowa muskrats living free and uninhibited, living as individuals and as social groups, living as their "own muskrats" though subject to Laws of Life. Further illustrating what we need to watch out for in philosophizing about Nature and her open book are some of the facts and figures that do not behave reassuringly in balance sheet tabulations.

Female muskrats of northern regions usually breed for the first time at ages of a little less than a year, or usually in the spring following their year of birth. Of nearly 5,000 young Iowa females examined after the breeding season, 74 or 1.5% had bred during the years of their own births, or at ages of three to five months. The averages of these precocious breeders among the season's young varied with the year, from none at all up to 5.3%. Two breeding seasons are about as many as our female muskrats are likely to have. Most of the females, if escaping traps, disease, and other perils of the flesh, begin to show aging after their second breeding season.

Our records of birth dates of about 3,000 litters of Iowa muskrats show that most young are born from May through July, with considerable numbers in April and August, and some even in March, September, and October. The breeding season is more apt to continue late at our latitude than to start early and it is essentially confined to the warmer months of the year. The occasional precocious breeding of young of the year helps to string out the breeding season into the fall.

Successive litters are born about a month apart to the ordinary north-central female during her annual breeding season. That does not mean that any one female gives birth to litters at monthly intervals from, let us say, April to September, nor, in places where the breeding is year-around, that any one female gives birth to 12 litters of muskrats in a year. (In Louisiana, where breeding takes place the year-around, Ted O'Neil reports the most breeding in November and March and the least breeding in July and August.)

The number of litters recorded per year for our adult females in Iowa varies from none at all to five.

Non-breeding females include some that are apparently past breeding ages, but, more commonly, they are potential breeders that live unmated in out-of-the-way places. They are to be found, for example, in small cattail "islands" out in the open water of some marshes—outside of lines of travel for prospective mates. Of samples totaling some 800 adult females for which seasonal breeding performances were traced on our Iowa areas, an average of 10% did not conceive young during the particular breeding seasons that were investigated. The average number of non-breeders among the adult females varied from as low as 3% to 7% for some years to as high as 19% to 21% for other years.

The approximately 1,000 adult females that we have studied in Iowa gave birth to an average of two-and-one-half litters per breeding season. About a fourth gave birth to four litters or more (five litters in two cases, or about a fifth of 1%) during an annual breeding season. In some years, almost no adult females would give birth to as many as four litters, and, in other years, it was evident that nearly half of them did.

Only one specimen of the precociously breeding young females gave birth to more than a single known litter during its birth year, and that one had two litters. Precocious young should not be expected to do much breeding, considering that they have their litter from late July into the fall, mostly in August and September. They just do not have it in them physically to be very prolific until they grow older, bigger, and have the favorable time of year for breeding ahead of instead of behind them.

On the other hand, the full-sized healthy adults often have breeding potential that is not converted into young muskrats, even when well-mated and well-fed. Here, we run into one of the things that mislead in the pencil-and-paper figuring.

No one need challenge the popular idea that the muskrat is a prolific rodent even as prolific rodents go. The species does have impressive powers of increase, specializing in mass production rather than in careful rearing. Our record of a female muskrat conceiving 46 young in a single year undeniably represents a busy home life, whether or not comparison is made with mass producers such as mice, rats, and rabbits. Nevertheless, a strong tendency toward restriction of breeding may be noted on the part of our Iowa muskrats whenever too much begins to look like too much for a given place at a given time.

Thus, for a marsh that is crowded according to muskrat standards of crowding, breeding may practically cease after the birth of a litter or two. This happens as early as early June, with little or no further breeding that year, the passing of the fine summer weeks, notwithstanding. Such an automatic check on reproduction is closely tied up with the numbers of young that get under foot and with the extent that these young appear to make the adults less concerned about their falling birth rates than about what else, if anything, up to and including peace, is worth having in life, anyway.

There is nothing about this self-limitation that represents any trend toward racial degeneration or any changed property of protoplasm or anything more irrevocable than passing through a large proportion of a breeding season without breeding.

Muskrat females giving birth to three or four litters during a breeding season are, as a rule, those having relief from overly close and continued association with their early-born. Any generalization that there is nothing like a big and increasingly unhappy family to discourage further mass production has its converse in that there is nothing like the young inhibitors ceasing their inhibiting to restore mass production.

The young inhibitors may have something tragic befalling them, something like a succession of late spring and early summer floods that drown at helpless stages most of the young born during the first half of the breeding season. In such cases, we can get some biological compensating of sorts that pencil-and-paper calculators seldom allow for when tinkering with balance sheet formulas. Some very severe juvenile mortality on our study areas *can* result in sufficient *extra* breeding—beyond the amount that otherwise would occur—to give us about as high a population of muskrats as would be tolerated anyway. I am not saying that the trappers would be delighted with larger proportions of low-value, August-born "kits" in their later fur catches, but, from the standpoint of balancing and counterbalancing in population numbers, Nature offsets, on the production line, much mortality in just such ways.

A more usual happening on a muskrat marsh is that a goodly proportion of the early-born young go to seek their fortunes in places where they, in their turn, do not feel quite so inhibited by their elders.

They do not go just anywhere. Rather, they go off 50 or 60 yards or so to the side of the "old homestead," to some quiet place having food and water and perhaps a vacant lodge or two and not too many other muskrats. With this local exodus of early young leaving the adults not quite so muskrat-conscious at all hours of the day, the third or fourth litters may arrive on schedule. The population may be thought of as up-and-coming and blessed with pioneering vigor. It is a reassuring picture of fertility and plenty when we see it, but we do not always see it. Something akin to a livable frontier is required for surplus animals to pioneer into, and muskrats are capable of filling up their Utopias as well as are most other forms of life.

With small litters or large litters, the muskrats have it in them to do about all the reproducing they need to do. The two main southern muskrats—the Maryland and Louisiana forms—have litters containing an average of only about four young, or fewer; yet these have given us some of the most extreme examples of top-heavy populations and destructive activities in their marshland environments. In north-central United States, I have virtually never seen, even on wildlife refuges untrapped for years, muskrat "eat-outs" having the destructiveness frequently seen in the coastal marshes of the South. Ted O'Neil estimates that an adult Louisiana female will have five or six litters in a year and that it is capable of having up to seven or eight. This would mean a total annual productivity of young that would be near our north-central average, but my view is that our north-central muskrats may be more prolific than the southern forms, year after year.

Muskrat litters vary greatly in size, from one to three for the smaller litters up to more than a dozen for the larger. Fourteen (from a German report) is the record number of young of which I know for one litter. In Iowa, we find a considerable number of litters of 11 young, but that is also our observed limit, so far, in nearly 2,700 litters for which we have information on sizes.

The late litters born to precocious females in the year of their own birth run a bit small, averaging about five young, or about five-eighths the size of the average litter for a full adult. Such litters from precocious young make up less than 3% of our recorded totals for Iowa litters. In our region, they usually can be ignored in balance sheet calculations, both from economic and biological points of view.

Some of the year-to-year differences in average sizes of litters conceived by adult muskrats appear to be meaningful. After statistical purification of our Iowa figures, we find a wave-like trend toward increases and decreases in average sizes. The crests and troughs of the waves line up fairly well with the high and low years of the hares and grouse in the northern parts of our region. From the "cyclic low" year of 1936, when the average size was 6.4, the averages increased to 8.2 and 8.4 for the "cyclic high" of 1941-42, gradually declined to 6.4 by the "cyclic low" of 1946, increased again to 8.2 by 1951, then turned downward once more, to reach 6.4 again by 1956.

Some differences in size of litters were attributed to local differences in population pressures and food resources, but these were apparently of minor significance compared with the unknown "cyclic" influences. The litters of adults in the more crowded and poorly fed populations, in general, were only slightly smaller than those of better situated adults.

*   *   *

Now that we have some of the ingredients of balance sheet equations, we can see how our muskrats may each

FIGURE 5. "In northern fur countries, trappers may just about *be* the public."
Photos by D. E. Denmark, Hudson's Bay Company.

FIGURE 6. "On the right kind of late fall day or night . . . muskrats may be caught by the hundreds or thousands . . ." Photo by Iowa State Conservation Commission.

Figure 7. "To set traps right, one should take advantage of muskrat psychology." Photos by M. L. Ferguson, Iowa State College.

year give birth to, even at their more modest breeding rates, many more young muskrats than their environments can well accommodate or more than their own kind may be expected to tolerate.

Obviously, there must be shaking down to fit, or we would soon be finding muskrats living or trying to live in peculiar places far more frequently and in far greater numbers than we do. The annual fur harvest eliminates many over-produced animals, but it is not invariably efficient in so doing, and there are places where no trapping is ever done. Yes, muskrats may move on occasion, but neither is migration the full answer. Some dying from natural causes has to be done somewhere by some young muskrats, whether they are cute, innocent, and potentially worth a dollar or two a piece, or otherwise.

The popular concept of "Balance of Nature" implies a smoother equilibrium between the forces of reproduction and mortality and different workings of the balancing mechanisms than is actually the case. There is balancing and counter-balancing in Nature's ways of doing things, but Nature can juggle her bookkeeping.

One may be accustomed to thinking of the "Balance of Nature" simply in terms of reproduction adding young muskrats to a population of adults and then mortality subtracting young (together with some old animals) to give a certain population as the remainder. One may think of every little change in food or enemies or birth rates as having its influence on the end product and of each subtraction of young cutting down the end product some more.

Think, instead, in terms of Nature figuratively making up her mind pretty much in advance about what she is going to have as an end product and manipulating the other figures accordingly. Think in terms of Nature doing a lot of substituting of one mortality factor for another—of muskrat teeth for mink teeth or fox teeth, of drought or drowning or disease losses for any kind of killing teeth. Think of Nature substituting new-born young for weaned young, of weaned young for new-born young or unborn young. Think of all of this, over and over again and vice versa, to make answers come out right.

Our long-term records for regularly studied Iowa areas show much definiteness in the mathematical patterns followed by the muskrat populations. If we look at our figures for this or that stretch of creek or river or drainage ditch, alone, without reference to neighboring areas, we may not see much if any evidence of a master pattern. But, if we total up what figures we have for 25 square miles or so of stream valleys, etc., and consider the combined area as we would a single land unit, we are more apt to see evidence of strong balancing trends that persist irrespective of many year-to-year differences in food and water conditions, differences in birth rates, and differences in other parts of the life equations of the muskrats. Similar illustrations of both Nature's leeway and rigidities are to be seen in records for other long-studied muskrat areas in the United States and Canada.

Unless something like a severe drought befalls them, muskrat populations may, for a few years, show essentially predictable rates of increase between spring and fall. Then, something happens reminding one of a shift of gears, and, for a time, we still see that a pattern is being followed, though a different pattern than before.

Some changes in the annual patterns line up with what we think of as "cyclic" changes. Other pronounced changes in muskrat populations accompany pronounced environmental changes, as when a cattail marsh loses its cattails and becomes an open-water lake, or when an open-water lake goes dry and then passes through a marshy stage as the water returns. At least, it is significant that population patterns may be clearly defined for years at a stretch.

In short, the mathematical patterns seem to be set chiefly by the amount of crowding that the muskrats themselves will put up with. This toleration toward crowding is influenced not only by the "cyclic" stages that already have been mentioned but also by the major features of the environment occupied by the muskrats.

The vital statistics from our muskrat areas indicate that, at *low* population levels for an area in good condition for muskrats, the rates of survival of the young that are born during a breeding season tend to be *high*. Inefficient breeding resulting from the difficulties that scarce muskrats may have in finding mates may still cut down the over-all rates of increase from the breeding population. For this reason, the over-all rates of increase tend to be *highest* for *moderately low* rather than for *very low* populations. Compared with what happens at crowded population levels, the muskrats not only produce more young and take better care of them at *moderately low* levels, but the young also do better at taking care of themselves—they can find more and better places for feeding and refuge and staying out of trouble. Heavy populations of minks and other formidable predators were observed to live in the midst of such comfortably situated muskrat populations without evidence that they were able to prey upon them.

The most successful rearing of young muskrats recorded during our Iowa field studies occurred on a tract of marsh diligently hunted over during the breeding season by minks. Over 80% of the total young conceived here at this time by the local female muskrats were present in the vicinity on the opening day of the trapping season in the fall. The case is especially noteworthy in that the three locally active and identifiable minks were individuals known for their decided taste for muskrat flesh, having "specialized" in scavenging upon muskrats that died from an epidemic of winter and spring. The minks ate muskrat flesh—some of it far along in decay—when they could get it, but they could do this only during the period when muskrats were dying from disease. In adjoining places where muskrats were not dying from disease, neither were they being fed upon by minks, despite the regular presence of the minks in these places.

When life is safe and easy for the muskrats of our better Iowa environments, adult females may successfully rear averages as high as 20 young per year, and averages of 12 to 15 are not unusual. Commonly, this means half to three-quarters of the young that are born—which still falls short of *all* of the muskrats that are born growing up into wearers of salable pelts. There is nothing like the latter in Nature's book, and there are reasons why not. When our fall muskrat populations get up to 20 to 30 per acre in the best of marshy growths, and up to 100 to 150 per mile along the more food-rich ditches and creeks, we have plenty of muskrats, irrespective of the many little muskrats that never grew up to be big ones.

Nature becomes increasingly prodigal of the lives of young muskrats as populations become increasingly heavy in relation to environmental limitations and the dispositions of the muskrats. Overcrowding alone may cut down the number of young reared to an average of less than a half-dozen per adult female, or about the equivalent of the young reared of a single litter.

At such times, entire litters may be killed by other muskrats shortly after weaning—sometimes before weaning. Late-born litters in particular may have hardly a chance of surviving. Constant frictions in crowded populations may result in much shifting of litters from place to place, with young being left behind and forgotten by their mothers, suckling litters being abandoned outright to starve or die of exposure, and with just about everything coming along in the way of the troubles besetting over-populations. In the event of a drought drying up an over-populated area, the troubles of the muskrats may be spectacularly aggravated.

Except during drought exposures, the young muskrats usually preyed upon by minks are the newly weaned that may be forced ashore by unhappy relations out where too many muskrats already live. Mother muskrats may kill two or three of their last litter while persuading them to leave home before the birth of the next litter in line. Youngsters may swim off to neighboring lodges only to find that the muskrats there also have teeth and more company than they care for. Feelings of being unwanted lead to lives of secrecy and watchfulness and crafty dodging, but muskrat psychology has resiliences, too, and most muskrat youngsters that learn hard things the hard way and live through it continue to stay where they know their way around or work into such neighborhood wet places as appear to be in lesser demand by their assertive elders. Comparatively few of the overproduced young seem to satisfy their impulses to get away from it all by choosing the attractive mink trails in the shore vegetation for their individual retreats.

From about midsummer on into the fall, the few minks that frequent the deeper parts of a muskrat marsh and the majority frequenting the shore zones have poor luck in eating young muskrats unless something disastrous happens to the muskrats. There may be windfalls, literally such, as when a storm beats down or washes lodges in to shore, to leave survivors of different ages temporarily marooned in the regular travel routes of the minks. The younger of these vulnerably situated muskrats are among the likeliest of mink victims. One mother mink, the food habits of which were followed, was not known to feed upon or to bring muskrats to her den either before or much after a violent storm, but, during or immediately afterward, she brought in 16 of the homeless young muskrats that were trying to sit out the crisis on land.

To a very considerable extent, mink predation tends to be centered upon the biological wastage of muskrat populations—upon individuals or parts of populations having slight chances of staying alive anyway under ordinary conditions. This is quite a different story from the general assumption that luckless muskrats lose their lives merely because the minks are there to eat them. It does not follow that, if the minks were not there to eat such muskrats, we should have by the next trapping season so many more muskrats to skin out of their fur coats.

*   *   *

Scavenging by minks and other flesh-eaters upon the bodies of muskrats may greatly complicate our understanding of predatory activities unless one is well acquainted with what disease is doing at the time. Fortunately, our field records are sufficiently complete for many periods of dying on Iowa marshes and watercourses so that evidences of predation can be satisfactorily separated from evidences of scavenging upon diseased dead. A very large proportion of the otherwise inexplicable cases of minks (and raccoons and foxes) feeding upon muskrats at times and places where the muskrats should be living securely from predators can be traced down to local dying of the muskrats from disease.

Predatory scavengers do not always find these diseased dead, nor any large proportion of them. In hot weather, tremendous numbers of disease victims decay without having anything larger than insects feeding on them. Sometimes, sick animals are killed by predators at different stages of their sickness. The clearest cases are of the sick either leaving places where they are safe from predators or attracting the notice of predators by their bumbling actions and so on. Suffering young may cry. Sometimes, also, some killing of healthy young results indirectly from local die-offs from disease, as when intelligent flesh-eaters start digging into muskrat retreats to reach the dead that they smell within and go on from there to develop habits of raiding nests containing any young that they can catch. Minks seem less apt to participate in this sort of activity than raccoons, pigs, and members of the dog family.

Unlike the usual workings of predation, disease *can be*, on occasion, so deadly as to leave little possibility for compensations. When a whole population collapses, one does not think in terms of a dead muskrat making room for another one to live—when the area has no others to take the place of the dead. And, when an area is so saturated with contagious disease that muskrats can not long live there even when they do come in, we may have something akin to a desert so far as muskrats are concerned.

Still, we get much compensating when disease losses are only locally severe. A local die-off may knock a big hole in the marsh population and then subside after a week or two. The dying of hundreds of animals may be offset by the filling in of the environmental vacancies by population surpluses having nowhere else to go. If the dying does not start up again, the marsh may soon be accommodating all of the muskrats that it has accommodations for, anyway.

*   *   *

So we see a great amount of variation in the so-called "limiting factors" at the same times that muskrat populations follow more or less set patterns. Our long years of records are most useful in helping to straighten up our thoughts on some complicated and obscure matters. When the statistics are down on charts, the ups and downs of an area's muskrat populations may show few if any connections with the year-to-year differences in kinds, numbers, and activities of predatory enemies and in the less drastic impacts of disease and weather. The slackening of breeding, catching up on losses, marking time, shifting populations, fighting or being tolerant, enduring and adjusting that muskrats do all seem to spell out for our north-central region: That the muskrat is its own chief limiting factor in relation to the environment in which it is adapted to live.

CHAPTER IV

Still More About Muskrats and What They Do and What Happens to Them

THE HEMORRHAGIC disease of muskrats can either look worse than it is or be worse than it looks. Although I do not think that anyone has as yet proved its exact cause, the disease is clearly infectious and seems to occur in nearly all parts of North America where muskrats live. It is *not tularemia,* though it often resembles tularemia in its liver spotting (Figure 3). It is unresponsive to the standard laboratory tests for tularemia. Certain common symptoms of the disease, such as external bleeding from natural body openings, are not typical for tularemia.

It is not by any means a disease restricted to cool or cold weather but it often starts up in late fall and cleans out the muskrats of a marsh (or of a sizable area of marsh) shortly before the trapping season opens. Or, if trapping is delayed until late winter or spring, not many living muskrats may be left in places having hundreds or thousands at freeze-up. It *can* be one of the most effective upsetters of trapping plans.

Furthermore, it is very possible for trappers or outdoorsmen to overlook or misinterpret the evidence of disease mortality. At times, dead muskrats lie on the mud or float about lodges and burrows in conspicuous numbers. At other times, most of the victims die out of sight in the lodges and burrows. One needs to be at the right place

49

at the right time and to know what to look for to detect some of these die-offs, even when they may be so deadly as to leave almost none of the animals alive on extensive marsh or stream areas.

The muskrats may suddenly not be there any more, and suspicious souls may contend that they were trapped before season. There can be, it is true, illegal trapping—some of it so clever as to be almost undetectable. Even the cleverest of "soonering," however, may leave some "sign" for experienced field observers to make out if they search for it. But whole tracts of muddy marsh, for example, may "go dead" in the space of about a week, without a track of a human foot or of a boat in places that no man could reach without tracking. Maybe, a muskrat body floats in a channel or another lies in the mud with only its back sticking out, softening, spreading, and blending with water and mud in the warm October sunshine.

Or the season may be midwinter. The lodges in one corner of a marsh have unrepaired mink holes and heaps of mink droppings consisting of muskrat remains. Heads, tails, feet, pieces of skin, and tufts of fur of muskrats are strewn about on ice or snow. Bodies are dragged from one mink retreat to another. Some muskrat bodies are piled up inside of lodges. Add to this, blood and mink trails everyhere, and it will look like the scene of wholesale murdering.

But in my snooping around and peeking into dark and smelly places when something went wrong with the muskrats, I sometimes found many dead muskrats that were untouched by minks. A Canadian friend told me that he has found as many as 18 dead of disease in a single lodge. My own record for a lodge is 11—found twice in one year.

These dead may be fresh enough or well enough preserved by freezing to reveal exactly what happened. Not only do their insides typically show the disease but their sexual development also provides a basis for estimating the time of death. Frequently, victims of early winter epidemics may remain refrigerated in their lodges until spring and still tell their story when examined. Again and again, we have thus traced back the periods of winter dying to those times when minks (sometimes dogs or foxes) were noted to display unusual interest in the lodges of a particular part of a marsh. In some areas of the West, coyotes specialize in digging into muskrat lodges in which they smell dead muskrats.

The minks are the real experts in locating and getting at the dead. They may systematically work from lodge to lodge over a marsh from freeze-up until spring. They may have other reasons, too, for entering lodges almost anywhere on a marsh. Fishes, frogs, water insects, etc., are to be found in or about the plunge holes. And the minks do very much like muskrat flesh and eat it when, where, and if they can.

As long as that muskrat flesh is capable of taking care of itself by slipping away through the water or by fighting back, the minks feed upon their fishes and frogs, perhaps upon dead waterfowl from the hunting season of the previous fall, or upon something that they catch or find dead on the surrounding land. How much the minks hope for the best in the course of their tireless quartering of a frozen-over muskrat marsh I cannot say, but when a mink does hit a jack pot of several dead and not-too-stale muskrats in a lodge it surely knows it.

In view of minkish habits concerning diseased muskrats, the question comes up as to whether the minks spread the disease. Theoretically, they could, for they may drag and cache bodies of diseased muskrats hundreds of yards from places currently being disease-swept. Such carcasses, and probably their corresponding remains in mink droppings, must be regarded as infective material. But the dozens of closely studied case histories of epidemics of the hemorrhagic disease among Iowa muskrats do not implicate minks in touching off new epidemics or in making old ones worse. Also theoretically conceivable is the possibility that the scavenging by the minks, by consuming so much infective material, may prevent epidemics from spreading. A realistic statement would seem to be that the minks ordinarily do not influence the course of the epidemics in one way or the other.

The agency that really can spread an epidemic of hemorrhagic disease in an area's population of muskrats is an infected muskrat. The muskrat may do this either while alive and moving about or as a body lying where it died in the living quarters, passageways, or feeding grounds of its healthy fellows. What we know about muskrats in this respect is sufficient so that we need not strain for explanations in terms of the contagion that *might* be carried by minks, by water birds, by hunters' boots and boats, by water currents and so on.

The Iowa case histories of epidemics show two notable trends of evidence. One trend relates to the starting of epidemics and the other to what epidemics may do after getting started.

Almost without exception, our local dying from the hemorrhagic disease starts up again after periods of quiescence at the same old places on a marsh or along a stream. At first, the muskrats may die almost nowhere else than in these old "hotspots," despite the muskrat bodies that the minks drag into holes and the hundreds of animals that die away from such old "hotspots" at the height of preceding deadly epidemics.

After the epidemics get started, they may then spread during the following weeks in just about any direction in which muskrat populations are present to promote the spreading. The course of spread of a big die-off plotted on a map can give an impression of concentric rings, as parts of populations collapse in their turn, farther and farther away from the original "hotspot" or the site of the first dying. A couple of weeks of this may depopulate whole tracts of a marsh within a radius of a quarter of a mile from a "hotspot."

Breaks in the distribution of a population—such as wide expanses of open water or distances of over two hundred yards between places occupied by muskrats—may stop, or at least impede, the spread of epidemics in some directions. Of course, when sick muskrats manifest their sickness by traveling away from their regular home ranges and head at random across a marsh or work for a mile or more along a shore zone, isolation from the site of a die-off becomes a relative and provisional matter.

But, natural isolation of population groups may set some limits to the areas likely to be covered by an epidemic. Moreover, some epidemics subside of their own accord while plenty of muskrats for them to kill still remain ahead of their lines of spread.

Hot weather terminates many spring die-offs from the hemorrhagic disease, though dying may start up again in fall at the old "hotspots" if these become repopulated by muskrats during the summer. My impression is that the rapid and thorough decay of muskrat bodies in midsummer is not conducive to spread of the disease. We do get midsummer epidemics, including some of extreme deadliness; but the general run of mid-summer victims show a pneumonic type of the disease, which is presumably air-borne from animal to animal. Most of the others dying from the hemorrhagic disease in midsummer do so in the old "hotspot" areas—perhaps at long intervals or at intervals just sufficient to continue revealing that these places are dangerous. Or, perhaps the dying ceases at the old "hotspots," and the muskrats build up there once more, perhaps laying the groundwork for something *BIG* with the coming of fall.

With 10 years or more of records on many examples of "hotspots," we should be entitled to do some generalizing. All of the "hotspots" that are clearly chronic over our Iowa study areas are in places where the muskrats come in regular or frequent contact with mud, but mud is not the sole answer. Infinitely more of the muddy retreats of muskrats are *not* proven (or suspected) "hotspots." Furthermore, the records indicate that the "hotspots" may retain deadly infectiousness for muskrats for at least five years in the total absence of muskrats, whether wet or drought-exposed for long periods or alternately wet and dried out.

Judging from records on the "hotspots" that have long been kept under observation, some "hotspots" may be limited to the vicinity of a single burrow system or to a little island of cattail, bulrush, or reed. Those with the most distinguishable boundaries may be tracts of less than a quarter of an acre or up to a couple of acres or more in size. A corner of one of our study areas has two notorious old "hotspots" separated by a smaller "safety island" on which dead muskrats are rarely found. One fall, a sizable group of muskrats suffered no detected disease mortality on the "safety island" at the time that the populations on both sides were collapsing. Totals of 22 and 29 dead were recorded for the respective sides of the "safety island" during that die-off, with no survival of muskrats in either "hotspot."

Other "hotspots" lack boundaries that can be definitely established from the information at hand. A marsh may have an area of four or five acres, in some part of which dying starts up almost every year when muskrats are in it to die. The same can be said of some narrow strip of shore zone 200 or 300 yards in length. Undoubtedly, there are parts of such tracts that have different degrees of infectiousness. My thought is that few parts of any marsh long occupied by muskrats in our north-central region are completely free from the hemorrhagic disease and that the worst "hotspots" tend to become that way because of the large numbers of muskrats dying in them over long periods.

I am not maintaining that the infectiousness of a "hotspot" can not run out in the absence of renewals if it has time enough to do it. I do not know how long infectiousness can last if unrenewed, but it conceivably could build up enough from new deaths alone to account for some of the local deadliness we see in old "hotspots." Certain of even the smaller "hotspots" had totals of up to 100 or more muskrats dying in them during a 10-year period. That spells out possibilities for concentrated infection.

Some of the population symptoms that I faithfully put down in my field notes long before I knowingly worked with the hemorrhagic disease now tempt me to speculate about what *may* have been happening 20 years or more ago in the way of poorly detected or undetected disease mortality at the sites of the present day "hotspots." There could have been a great deal.

Nothing that I can see in either the clearest evidence or in the most plausible of speculations concerning the persistence of infectious "hotspots" of the hemorrhagic disease would seem to offer much comfort to persons who would like to have the "hotspots" tame down and be good, henceforth and permanently. I am afraid that bad "hotspots" have it in them to remain bad almost indefinitely.

Our best-studied "hotspots" commonly have some special features to attract muskrats year after year: good food and water conditions plus the correct "lay of the land" and the evidences of former occupancy by muskrats that muskrat newcomers find reassuring. Nothing compares with pleasant surroundings and a nice vacant apartment in the form of old channels and burrows and chambers to invite home-seeking muskrats to tarry and rehabilitate and settle and die.

These death-traps are a main reason why serious dying may continue on a marsh at times of low populations of muskrats. Because of their attractiveness, they may draw muskrats away from the safer places, and, the more muskrats are attracted to them to die, the deadlier they may be expected to become. On our study areas, we have "hotspots" so deadly that muskrats hardly stay alive in them for more than a few weeks—if as long as that—at any time of the year.

One "hotspot" of about an acre was the starting point of a spring epidemic that killed about 400 muskrats and almost wiped out the muskrats wherever it spread. Despite the fact that 20 to 25 dead per acre were found in the wet-marsh tracts having the heaviest mortality, the only place in the vicinity showing deadliness in later years was the old "hotspot," itself. The dying over most of the area spread into by this epidemic did not happen to leave many dead in any one place likely to be used by muskrats in later years—not even the sites of dying of whole groups of muskrats in particular lodges. In contrast, the "hotspot" had enough allure and a strategic enough location so that some muskrats were almost certain to be moving into it from time to time or to start housekeeping conveniently close by.

FIGURE 8. "The most effective open water fall trapping . . . put a muskrat in practically every trap." Photos by M. L. Ferguson, Iowa State College.

FIGURE 9. "About all that most victims can do when caught in stop-losses is to wriggle backward, and, if there is sufficient water for drowning . . . they stand a good chance of drowning in it." Photos by M. L. Ferguson, Iowa State College.

After years of seeing our Iowa muskrat populations collapsing whenever epidemics caught up with them, I found, in the fall of 1950, that not only were few muskrats dying on the study areas but also that certain populations were showing both high rates of infection and high rates of recovery from the hemorrhagic disease. On one big marsh, probably most of the resident muskrats, old and young, were contracting the disease, yet hardly any were dying from it. Only in old "hotspots" was evidence found of any dying at all, and not many dead ones were found there. When opened up for examination, the bodies of those that did die of the disease often showed evidence of repeated infections. Their livers had disease lesions of different sizes and in all stages of freshness and healing. Some victims had dead tissue and scars and pus pockets representing up to a quarter of the volume of the liver. It takes considerable time for all of that to happen in a muskrat's body—weeks, maybe months.

The one period of such evidently strong resistance to the disease for which we have the best information lasted somewhat over two years, from the midsummer of 1950 past the midsummer of 1952. It was, at the same time, a period of large average sizes of muskrat litters, of precocious breeding by young females in the calendar years of their own birth, and of general behavior signifying contentment, well-being, and unusual ability to tolerate crowding and emergencies. Muskrats did continue to die from the pneumonic type of the disease much as it hit them, even in 1951 when the commoner types were not doing a great deal more than mildly spotting up livers of the animals contracting them. (I am not sure that muskrats ever do have any effective resistance to the hemorrhagic disease if it gets a good start in their lungs, whether their general resistance is high or not.)

Then, some time after midsummer 1952, the muskrats

seemed to lose their exceptional resistance to the disease. The animals contracting the disease were dying about as they had been in the spring of 1950 and showing about the amount of liver spotting that could be expected to develop in a week or a few days longer.

During 1946, 1947, and 1956, most muskrats dying from the disease showed evidences of dying from hemorrhages before liver lesions had much chance to develop. In many cases, the victims surely could not have stayed alive more than a few days after infection. These years were all characterized by small average litter sizes, lack of precocious breeding, and much restlessness and social intolerance in the muskrat populations.

*   *   *

Most of the muskrats that one notices doing something conspicuously individualistic seem to be the older ones, or, if not really the old, the middle-aged—at any rate, those that get to be big, husky, and as much their own bosses as muskrats get to be. Possibly many young and small ones may have similarly individualistic ideas without living long enough to show their individuality. To become a super muskrat, a young muskrat's first job is to grow up. Let him (or her) put on three or four pounds of what counts and grow a thick skin and a front end that can bite through things before he (or she) ventures forth for impressive deeds.

These muskrats are not being held up here as examples for other muskrats or for any other creatures. They are not necessarily good citizens even as muskrats. Their claims to special recognition are simply that they did things that were recognizably special, by any standards of durability, venturesomeness, independence, persistence, dominance, or piracies that are applicable to muskrats.

It can hardly be proved that the enterprising giant musk-rats have more me-first philosophies than have the runts that develop quickness on the dodge and propensities for sneaking in and eating the hindquarters off one of mamma's newly born darlings when mamma is not home, but the giants can better afford to disregard public opinion.

One such giant was known to circulate about the frozen surface of a dried-up marsh, breaking into lodges still having muskrats in residence and killing and eating the occupants. It was more adept at this than were the couple of local minks that fed mainly on muskrats dying from cold and hunger. Possibly the victims, while properly wary concerning the minks, were not expecting exactly that conduct on the part of a fellow muskrat.

Ordinarily, the property-owners, the confident and right-ful possessors of muskrat equivalents of legal and moral rights, have the advantage in encounters with outsiders whenever unpleasantness does occur. Fighting between social unequals, when taking place, tends to become almost ritualistic. After preliminary passes at each other's faces or forequarters by both animals, the trespasser makes a run to escape, and the victorious resident pursues and endeavors to remove a bite of meat from the departing hindquarters while the opportunity lasts. The big cannibal of the dry marsh did not bother about the rules and ap-parently did not need to.

Occasionally, big ones that know their way around work drought-exposed Iowa marsh bottoms in all but the coldest weather. They feed most of the winter on rootstocks of rushes and cattails sticking out of the ice or snow or from the dry outer surfaces of the muskrat lodges. Some of these animals are tough characters. They may be treated respectfully by the minks of the neighborhood, including big and muskrat-hungry minks. By midwinter, they may use up their luck and resources, and the minks finally eat their thin and frozen bodies.

Or some get through. They gnaw their tails as these freeze—doubtless not pleased about it but still retaining some potentialities as living muskrats and willing to accept life for what it is as long as they have it. Or, those having all that they need of a combination of luck, smartness, toughness, and bigness may survive a hard winter in the very wide open spaces without losing so much as a tail tip.

Where two enormous old-timer muskrats meet on a dry marsh bottom and explore questions of what, how much, and why, there may be fur and droppings and red and yellow stains and scratched up snow or mud over an area of a square yard or two. A bounding trail may lead away, signifying that something has been settled. An animal long accustomed to having its own way may be presumed to feel some frustration when finding itself the recipient of a licking, but the consequences thereof can be more than psychological. An animal thus beaten in a hard fight may leave a trail ending in a smear of blood at a hole in ground or ice or muskrat lodge and never come out again.

Some of the most savage battles between such old-timers appear to have no relationship to necessity. Few of them look as if they could not have been avoided if either muskrat had conducted itself tactfully. So far as I can judge, this kind of fighting is not for food, for mates, or for pleasure. It has the marks of uninhibited short-temperedness, of collisions between head-strong and self-centered private enterprises.

Feats of arriving somewhere or of staying alive somewhere are notably accomplishments of old and big muskrats, whether fighting occurs or not. I know of a big one that wandered off across miles of desert, in which it found an isolated spring amid a four-acre patch of bulrushes; and here it lived in a concentration place for coyotes until dying of old age the year after. Big muskrats are conspicuous among those holing up in moist tiles or culverts or badger diggings, or those building lodges out of dirt, coarse weeds, and corn stalks in bottomland fields, or those leaving tracks in the dusty beds of small creeks, ditches, and brooks during droughts. During normal years characterized by little up-or-downstream movements of muskrats from summer to fall and into the winter, the muskrats that do undertake the unusual in going places and doing things seem at times to consist almost wholly of big ones.

The big muskrats displaying such independent inclinations may be of either sex, but those that I examine are usually males—which is a probable explanation for the known fact that adult males have more limited life expectancies than have adult females. Either sex may be in "prime of life" or past it; either may show old fight scars or none; either may make bad guesses in strategies of living. After becoming very big, the muskrats of either sex may find themselves behind more and bigger biological eight-balls than many of the younger, smaller, and more cautious of their fellows. They may have touchy, unsocial, and anti-social dispositions and no sense of obligation toward anyone or anything.

But the big ones, having in common only size and constitutional toughness, may still be the last ones alive on a marsh (or conceivably in a whole region) at the end of a drought crisis. They may be the only muskrats able to reach and pioneer in outlying places. They include females carrying unborn litters of young, which they may give birth to and rear far away from places regularly occupied by muskrats—in the pools of gravel pits, or roadside ditches, in springs or tile flows, in field ponds, in headwaters.

*   *   *

Springtime, a season of year well-known for the changes
it means in the behavior of animal life, may affect the out-
looks and fortunes of individual muskrats. In fact, the
muskrats may be responding to the changes of spring inside their lodges and burrows for weeks while the weather
is still winter outside. There may be plenty of food and
water and room to move around in if considered solely
in terms of what was adequate earlier. There may be fewer
other muskrats to compete with by spring than there were
in early winter, and those other muskrats may not be competing appreciably more for the essentials of life than they
did before. Or may they, if one considers more what an
animal *claims* rather than what it uses? Psychologically,
along with their glandular changes of the breeding season,
the muskrats become increasingly dissatisfied with having
a lot of other muskrats around. There may be much less
irritability than restlessness in the early spring muskrat
populations, much less of driving out than of wanting to
get out. When big spring dispersals away from wintering
quarters begin, very few of the hundreds or thousands of
muskrats participating on a local scale may have fight
wounds on their bodies. Neither may the animals that keep
popping out on the ice every time that a late-winter thaw
encourages them to do so have many fight wounds. Fight
wounds may come later in great profusion as unwelcome
visitors try to muscle in on the staked claims of residents,
but the annual exodus of surplus animals from wintering
quarters can look remarkably voluntary and bloodless.

A north-central muskrat population may show anything
but uniformity in sexual development in late winter and
early spring, and the fact that small and immature animals
are among the early ones to leave their wintering quarters

proves that the cause of their leaving is not wholly sexual restlessness. Absence of wounds on the bodies of these dispersing immatures suggests further that such animals are not necessarily subject to violence on the part of muskrats that are much farther along in breeding condition. My thought is that perceptive animals sense antagonisms of their fellows long before attacking stages are reached and that, even in the darkness of lodges and burrows under thick coverings of ice and snow, they take hints from sounds, odors, or body contacts. I feel sure that, at least in spring, many muskrats have the discretion to get out of places having prospects for trouble with their fellows well ahead of serious blow-ups.

Places that are suitable for wintering muskrats are usually suitable for breeding and rearing territories. If competition is slight, most muskrats show tendencies to breed at or near where they winter—we have both field observations and information on marked animals to back us on this point. As competition increases, smaller proportions of the wintering populations stay to breed where they wintered if they have any choice about it.

I do not know why certain muskrats remain in their wintering quarters to breed and why certain ones leave. Those remaining could be the first making up their minds to do so. They might also include those that are simply left in possession after the others pull out. Sometimes, the earliest territories to be definitely maintained have the earliest young; sometimes, they do not.

What a lot of this adds up to is that no one should assume that a tract of good muskrat environment can accommodate as many grown-up, enterprising, and functional muskrats in the spring as it did in late fall and early winter, even though food and water conditions remain favorable in the spring. Nor is there room for as many up-and-coming muskrat identities on the same tract in late fall and early winter as during the weeks of peace and lushness of late summer and early fall. Whether the shifts may be slow or rapid, the *annual* cycle of a muskrat population runs through three prominent leveling-off stages. Other expressions, such as thresholds of security or carrying capacity of an area for muskrats may be applied with reference to the leveling-off phenomena, but no one should, in so doing, think too much in terms of environment and not enough in terms of muskrats. The changes in physiology and psychology of the muskrats in the course of the year determine to a large extent how much and what kinds of environment the muskrats find acceptable.

CHAPTER V

Mostly About Practicalities in the Management of Northern Muskrats

Management, as the term is used here, can have numerous special connotations, depending upon what man intends in handling muskrat populations for his own purposes. Management suggestions in this book are not always labeled as such, nor, as the reader may have noticed in the earlier chapters, are they at all restricted to specific sections. This chapter is prepared in the hope of clearing up some of the questions the reader might like to have cleared up before he goes on to the trapping chapters—which have their own management aspects.

Management of muskrats may be direct, indirect, or incidental to something else. It may be to increase fur production or to extirpate muskrats from a locality or a region or simply to leave them unmolested on a wildlife refuge. It may be almost anything centering upon problems of what to do about muskrat damage, muskrat pelts, muskrat meat, muskrat diseases, muskrat enemies, muskrat habitats, muskrat trapping, or muskrat management in relation to fish management or to waterfowl management or to some other form of land use.

This chapter will be devoted much more to management of the muskrat as a resource than as a pest, but let us first consider its management as a pest.

* * *

When muskrats arouse human displeasure, they usually do it through eating or digging in ways that should be regarded as natural for muskrats behaving like muskrats.

Their eating is seldom more than a relatively minor offense against human economics, although it may not seem minor to persons depending for a livelihood upon small acreages subject to raiding by muskrats. The severest losses of this sort of which I know in North America are suffered by truck gardeners or farmers having delectable food plants growing adjacent to food-poor muskrat streams. Marsh-dwelling muskrats of our north-central region are not so likely to damage field crops unless large numbers are forced ashore by emergencies or population tensions. They usually have more attractive food resources where they live than on adjacent lands.

It is the propensity of muskrats to dig that makes them so unpopular in irrigation districts or where there are levees or earth dams or road grades to undermine. The animals may also plug tile flows with mud or vegetation, heap debris in boat houses, and be troublesome in other ways. They may even seem to do things out of cussedness, but it should be remembered that they are only animals with what we could call a lot of time on their hands and certain inclinations to keep occupied, somehow.

Management of the muskrat as a pest may consist either or both of trying to keep the animals killed off or trying to prevent living ones from doing damage. To anyone expecting to undertake controlling pest muskrats anywhere or at any time, I would make a first and elementary suggestion: find out what is legal.

Where and when it is desirable to keep muskrat populations as much reduced as possible, trapping should be as effective as any method in common use. Some of the methods described in Chapters VII and VIII are suitable for control trapping, so I shall not do more here than to express generalities.

Although cage-type live-traps may be used by some trappers, their greater bulkiness and uncertainties of action may all but rule them out of control programs unless it is important or necessary to take animals uninjured. This leaves us virtually dependent upon steel traps (including the improved designs such as "stop-losses") in our control trapping.

One difficulty in using steel traps for controlling muskrats during the warmer months is that many of the places most attractive to muskrats may be at the same time attractive to creatures other than muskrats. To avoid catching waterfowl, for example, trap sites should be chosen with care and the traps taken up or sprung as soon as it becomes no longer necessary to keep them set.

Systematic destruction of burrows should be carried on in places where no muskrats are wanted, for the old "vacant apartments" are special invitations for adjusting or wandering newcomers. Unless the burrows are in steep river banks or lead under and between glacial boulders or tree roots or are otherwise inaccessible, the more newly constructed systems may be dug out with hand tools. Many of the new systems have chambers only a short distance beneath the surface of the ground—even when dug into embankments. The longer a burrow system has been established, the more complex and relatively more impregnable it is likely to be.

Away from the truly "problem areas" where ditches and impoundments are so vulnerable to muskrat damage that muskrats must be relentlessly killed the year around, it may be possible to prevent damage in other ways. A small earth dam along a heavily-used migration route of muskrats might be better protected by galvanized wire mesh and rocks rather than by trying to kill every muskrat that comes near it, year after year. Muskrat-proofing is not always possible or may be too expensive, but a great deal of the prospective trouble from muskrats can be avoided by good planning.

So far as specific instructions for muskrat-proofing of dams or banks are concerned, the literature affords us only limited help, though I know that much experimenting has been done, especially by personnel of the U. S. Soil Conservation Service and some other public agencies. Most authors advise frequent inspections and prompt repairs whenever damage may be found, and some recommend constructions or devices or repellants to discourage or prevent animals from burrowing.

Tile drains may be protected from muskrats, and I have seen several good methods in use on Iowa farms. Tiles may be installed so that the flowing ends are out of reach of the muskrats. Or, the ends may be fitted with hinged metal lids that are heavy enough to stay closed when not forced open by water pressure. One of the cheapest and most practical of devices is a sheet-iron hanging cover with a piece of scrap iron welded to it for weight; a farmer-trapper who uses these on his tiles assured me that they worked perfectly in letting the water flow and in keeping the muskrats out.

*   *   *

Artificial propagation and stocking of muskrats are among the topics concerning which I have gotten many inquiries in the course of my studies.

Muskrats *can* be raised in captivity by skilled handlers, but get-rich-quick dreams of raising tremendous numbers in this way have had their awakenings in failure after failure. The dreams continue to tempt people who become preoccupied with the fecundity and pelt value of these fur-bearers and who make assumptions that do not hold up. No one has, to my knowledge, succeeded in making pen-raising of muskrats profitable as a fur-producing enterprise. Captive animals have not reproduced normally in the pens and they have shown great intolerance of crowding and restraint. However, "rat ranching," or encouraging muskrats to breed under essentially natural conditions, is quite a different thing and will be taken up farther on in this chapter.

The muskrat has been one of the species with which much stocking or transplanting has been done, but I think that all ventures of this sort should be undertaken with caution. Even if introduction of the species into a new place seems to invite no economic risks, there remains the need for considering natural values that may suffer as a result. There may be rather subtle questions as to what wildlife really belongs or does not belong in a given part of the world, and the person who would introduce exotic animals should always have the burden of proof. Tampering man need not forever be shifting plant or animal life over the earth's surface in the name of management or anything else, and we, collectively, have already made enough mistakes doing this to strive for more responsibility in future ventures.

Artificial restocking of native muskrat range after cataclysmic losses may have some management advantages, but it should be remembered that muskrats do have considerable ability to get around under their own power during spring dispersals and late-summer and early-fall adjustments. As I look over my notes on Iowa areas, I can see only a few cases where artificial restocking might well have been good management. All were in the springs of those years when local marshes were in good condition for muskrats yet without muskrats—or without more than trifling numbers. Other advantageous restocking might have been done in parts of the Dakotas following the droughts of the

Thirties, or farther west, where local crises wiped out the muskrats of isolated marshes.

A native population of muskrats that is greatly reduced from some severe emergency may still have far more muskrats left to breed than the number that any person or agency would be likely to obtain for replenishment. For the 1934-57 period of the Iowa investigations, the poorest "muskrat years" following the severest of droughts had state-wide populations estimated at 30,000 to 50,000 at the beginning of each breeding season.

Upsets in the social order of many species of mammals and birds through introductions of strange individuals into places having populations of established residents have been observed both in the out-of-doors and in laboratory experiments. For a species having a muskrat's disposition, increased social tensions surely could nullify advantages expected from stocking where strangers were dumped in the midst of populations that did not want them and would not tolerate them.

Transplants of wild animals for the stated purpose of "introducing new blood" have been made with game species almost everywhere that the public has attempted management. Undoubtedly, matings between close relatives often occurred among the muskrats of the Iowa observational areas, but there is much natural shuffling of hereditary potentialities during seasonal adjustments.

It should not be assumed that inbreeding must be invariably detrimental. Thriving forms of muskrats in central North America have survived great regional droughts during which lines of genetic continuity passed through small numbers of individuals. Colonization of central Europe by muskrats is reported to have gained its original impetus from the introduction of only three females and two males. Within a decade, their descendants were estimated in the millions—there can be no doubt that they thrived, close relationships notwithstanding. After all, we have in the muskrat an evolutionary product that got along for a long, long time without "blood renewals" through human intervention. Nature's ways of doing things may look casual to us, but she gets results, too.

If stocking of muskrats is decided upon, all efforts should be made to obtain animals that are in good health. To avoid mongrelizing native wildlife, the animals to be released should be of the same subspecies belonging in or living nearest to the area in which the stocking is to be done. The numbers stocked should be adequate for a breeding start—let us say a dozen per 100 acres for suitable but muskrat-vacant marshes in our north-central region. Releases should be only at times of year when newcomers could establish themselves, preferably in late spring, when so much restocking of muskrats occurs naturally.

*　　*　　*

It is evident why a valuable and easily-trapped fur-bearer may need appropriate legal protection. Legal protection, however, may be either wise or unwise. Good laws and poor laws reflect the inequalities of human endeavor, and the poorest laws may be a compounding of ineptitudes, political tinkering, pointlessness, and error buttressed by penalties.

Following are suggestions as to regulations that I think should work in the interests of better muskrat management.

I should advise against legislatures enacting *in detail,* or without making allowance for changing situations, the game or fur laws under which muskrats may be legally harvested. Legislatures may properly lay down the *broad framework* of game or fur laws, but, in my opinion, details and necessary modifications should be left so far as possible to qualified administrators.

There should be sufficient leeway in trapping regulations to permit needed modifications within subdivisions of a state or other political unit. I am aware of the administrative simplicity of having a fur season entirely open or entirely closed on a state-wide basis. But, when a large part of a state may have only remnant populations of muskrats concentrated in drought-shrunken puddles at the same time that another part may have heavy populations living in excellent environment, oversimplified administration can mean bad management.

Basically, there is sufficient resilience in muskrat populations to offset many mistakes in the law codes, and I do not feel that *extremely* close regulation of the means or extent of harvesting muskrat pelts is necessary. The biggest legislative objectives in this respect should be to prevent muskrats from becoming either too scarce or too abundant for their environment, to restrict the harvest to times when the pelts are commercially valuable, and to discourage the less satisfactory of harvesting methods, especially those methods that are needlessly wasteful, cruel for the muskrats, or inequitable for the public. Legislation must be workable, for its effectiveness depends not only upon enforcement but also upon what the public can be persuaded to do voluntarily.

My own views as to what should be the best times of year for harvesting muskrats are chiefly reserved for the trapping chapters, but I shall here propose one generalization: If the state conservation departments ever try to come to an agreement as to a uniform opening date for muskrat trapping to reduce smuggling of illegal furs across state lines, the first of December might be as good a compromise for an opening date as any. Pelts taken over most

FIGURE 10. "One-toe grips almost never hold a muskrat in the jaws of a common steel trap . . . but in stop-losses . . . may be about as effective as the more secure grips, even when the victims remain alive." Photos by M. L. Ferguson, Iowa State College.

FIGURE 11. "If trapping is attempted during the time between open water and freeze-up . . ." Photo by Iowa State Conservation Commission.

of the United States would by then be in fair to very good marketable condition.

The length of the open season should conform to the objectives sought in regulating the muskrat harvest. On marshes where a great problem is *undertrapping,* where "eat-outs" by muskrats may be a threat to extensive tracts of wetlands, a long season may be a management necessity. Elsewhere, muskrat populations may be practically cleaned out in less than a week if open water or other conditions favor the trappers as the season opens. Frequently, the status of a muskrat population may be only "so-so"—too many muskrats to justify closure but not enough to withstand ordinary intensities of exploitation—and then the difficulties of making administrative decisions may be considerable.

Restrictions of fur harvests through quotas and refuge systems should also allow sufficient administrative leeway to meet varying conditions. The setting of muskrat quotas to be taken from an area presupposes information as to the numbers of animals present and the proportions that should be harvested—and such information is not always to be had, even in approximate figures. If winter-killing or epidemics reduce the populations far below the quotas allowed, quotas obviously will not afford much protection. This is especially a possibility in northern regions where trapping is done in spring. In extreme cases involving either unforeseen losses or faulty estimates, trappers have taken about all of the available muskrats and still filled only small fractions of their quotas. At other times, rigid quotas have terminated the trapping while the population levels of the animals were much higher than needed for breeding stock—or, worse, while they were still undesirably high from the standpoint of sound management.

Our Iowa experiences with fur refuges on State-owned

marshes justify concluding that refuge systems *can* be of value in muskrat management, though not overmuch should be expected of them. These refuges had the purpose of giving legal protection to well-situated parts of muskrat populations in order that overflow animals would restock trapped-out neighboring parts during the spring dispersal. Their effectiveness varied with public sentiments and enforceability of regulations, with disease situations and adequacy of wintering environment, with year-to-year differences in behavior of the muskrats, with the actual needs for conserving breeding stock, and so on.

From my own experience, I think that restricting the number of muskrat traps allowed per trapper might be desirable, but a trap-limit should not be forced on the public in an arbitrary manner, without reference to circumstances. Where trapping in the lodges is done in late winter or early spring on a northern marsh, two or three dozen traps might be plenty for one man to take care of. When I had a young man's stamina and trapped on fairly good South Dakota marshes in the early Twenties, I never found that I could handle more than 50 muskrat traps efficiently. I also know that some expert Iowa trappers of the present day have concluded about the same thing. But, a great deal depends upon *how* the trapping is done, whether setting a large number of traps does or does not mean neglectful practices. (Ted O'Neil, who certainly has worked where muskrats are trapped, considered a legal maximum of 250 traps suitable for the average Louisiana marsh trapper under normal conditions, but felt that superior trappers could advantageously use 400 or more traps at sites of muskrat concentrations toward the end of the trapping season.)

Regulations prescribing the minimal distances that traps may be set from muskrat lodges have some point when the trapping season coincides with the breeding season of the muskrats, when trapping in or too near the lodges exerts a selective pressure upon the breeding females. On northern marshes, where the breeding has long been over by late fall and early winter, the muskrats occupying the lodges represent a cross-section of the population; and, for these marshes, I would say that regulations forbidding fall and winter sets close to the lodges are an unjustifiable nuisance, unless the muskrats really need extra protection from the trappers.

*   *   *

Campaigning against predatory enemies is one of the oldest of panaceas resorted to by the public in its efforts to increase populations of favored wildlife.

The extremes to which so-called "vermin control" may be carried on may have the flavor of religious persecution or similar fanaticism, with the killing being punishment for wild animals having predatory habits or for their "badness" in coveting what man has claimed for himself. There can be sadism behind such extremes, or a desire to kill for sport, or "business is business" motivations and prideful claims of common sense.

Although the common sense reasoning usually advanced has variable overtones, it has a most convincing simplicity: If a predator kills a muskrat, that means one less muskrat to be taken by the trapping; hence, if predators are killed before they kill muskrats, that means more muskrats to be taken by the trapping. The fallacies underlying much of this reasoning result from failures to take into account the automatic adjustments that are commonplace in the vital statistics of the muskrats. These adjustments and natural compensations have already been introduced in Chapters II, III, and IV, and there is more about them awaiting in Chapter IX, in the discussion of minks and mink trapping.

I may therefore skip the details and go on to emphasize

that the killing of muskrats by predators does not necessarily mean a poorer fur harvest, nor any actual loss in muskrat management even if money-making is the sole purpose of management.

It should be remembered that what the killing of a muskrat by an enemy often means is, in effect, that another muskrat's chances for living are thereby improved. The different agencies of mortality, including predation, do a lot of substituting for one another. The muskrat population that is harvestable by trappers seems to be determined *primarily* by how many muskrats the muskrats themselves will tolerate in relation to their living quarters, food, etc. On the whole, a sound philosophy of management would be to look upon predation as more of a *symptom* than a *cause* of something being wrong with a muskrat population—at least in those parts of the north-central region with which I am familiar.

The mink is the predator toward which muskrat trappers show the most animosity in this region, but it gets so much space in other chapters of the book that I shall not do much more than to mention it here.

If I had the responsibility of managing a north-central marsh for muskrats, I should wish to have a relatively high population of minks along with the muskrats. The mink as a species has been a most useful "barometer" of the well-being of the muskrat populations on my study areas, and I can recall almost no situations on these areas in which I felt convinced that muskrat management would have been materially aided by elimination of the minks.

Surely, someone may say, there must be circumstances under which selective predator control could have at least some advantage in muskrat management on at least a local scale. That I think is true, and, by looking over my case histories of muskrat populations, I can pick out a very few examples where deliberate campaigning against certain predators probably would have meant a more profitable fur harvest.

The most conspicuous case was one in which the specialized hunting techniques of a family of red foxes on drought-exposed muskrats reduced a population of between 250 and 300 to about 200 by the beginning of the trapping season. In other cases, clever and persistent domestic dogs learned to hunt muskrats and in so doing exerted pressures that seemed to cut slightly into otherwise secure muskrat populations. In recent years, depredations of raccoons upon helpless litters of young muskrats have aroused many trappers of eastern and southern coastal marshes, and I can see how a general habit of raiding muskrat nests on the part of abundant raccoons *could* be a problem in the management of muskrats of shallow marshes. On my Iowa study areas, however, this type of nest raiding was noted only in disease "hotspots."

Among miscellaneous predators, horned owls, snapping turtles, and nothern pike are traditionally thought by trappers to be serious muskrat enemies. The voluminous data we have on horned owl food habits in the north-central region revealed slight owl predation upon muskrats unless the latter were unusually vulnerable. So far, I have studied no situations in which I felt anything was to be gained in muskrat management by putting up pole traps for or shooting any predatory birds. Nor have I ever seen evidence supporting the antipathies of trappers toward snapping turtles as muskrat enemies—we have had quite "normal" productivity of muskrats on north-central marshes that literally crawled with snapping turtles. With respect to predation upon muskrats by northern pike, there can be remarkable local differences—the only severe case that I know about was in one area during one breeding season of the muskrats. The heaviest pike population that I ever saw in a northern Iowa marsh did not prevent the muskrats from increasing up to their highest level of which I have record for that marsh—up to between 3,200 and 3,400 on a 300-acre tract, as of late fall.

The significance of predatory mammals digging into muskrat lodges is hard to judge through casual observations. Commonly, the diggers are minks, but other predators or scavengers, such as hogs, coyotes, badgers, and bears, may do it here and there. Unless occurring during drought crises or at times when helpless young muskrats may be found in the nests, it seems to result in little actual mortality for muskrats of central North America. When there is much of this digging, the diggers may be presumed to find it profitable, whether they are attracted by muskrat victims of local die-offs, by lodge-dwelling mice, or by fishes congregated in plunge holes.

It is pertinent to ask what may be the effects on the muskrats of such digging into their habitations, even when the diggers do not succeed in catching muskrats. The answer depends upon whether the disturbances exceed the usually ample limits of tolerance of the muskrats. Well-situated muskrats on central and northern Iowa marshes have been able to adjust indefinitely to moderate disturbances, as from mink intrusions. Prompt and effective rehabilitation of damaged lodges may often be seen in mild winter weather, and cold weather may not place an insuperable handicap on the muskrats as long as materials for repairs (wet mud or vegetation) are available. However, extensive damage to lodges or burrows during droughts or freeze-outs may leave the animals with too few alternatives for adjustments. Too much can be too much.

In concluding this section, I would say that, rather than overemphasizing predator control, north-central muskrat managers would do better if they forgot about it as a management tool.

It has been earlier pointed out and may here be reiterated that, under normal living conditions, the predation suffered by the muskrats is chiefly an accompaniment of the natural shaking down to tolerable population levels during or shortly after the breeding season. There is then much population wastage that must necessarily always remain wastage, insofar as it is linked with the psychology of the muskrats, themselves. The most expendable parts of muskrat populations are not likely to be conserved for human use until the prime-fur months merely through unimaginative killing of the predators that, incidental to the overall wasting, may eat wastage muskrats.

In addition to having futilities, overemphasis on predator control in muskrat management can have its disadvantages. From the economic standpoint, alone, it may not only prove costly to carry on and costly in loss of revenues from other fur-bearers but it also may be costly in indirect ways. It can be conducive to scapegoat philosophies. It can lead to so much preoccupation with measures that do not count as to reduce the effective management that could be accomplished with similar expenditures of time and effort.

For another thing, excesses in campaigning against predators can alienate a part of the public that otherwise might be disposed to give muskrat management—as a legitimate form of wildlife management—encouragement and cooperation. Some of us feel that there is, or should be, more wildlife on earth than muskrats and more to wildlife management than making money out of muskrats or out of any managed or pampered species. A person having broad interests in the out-of-doors should not be expected to look pleasantly upon a beautiful marsh being made into a year-around death-trap for every flesheater that flies, walks, crawls, or swims, and he may ask just who owns the public's wildlife?

Extremes of predator control should seldom be necessary in muskrat management or in any kind of wildlife management that is intelligently and decently carried on.

* * *

Effective muskrat management is nearly synonymous with managing the environment in most regions where the species is valued as a fur-bearer. The north-central trapping public well knows that a marsh full of cattails, bulrushes, and duck potatoes, and having the right amount of water, may support thousands of muskrats per square mile, whereas a rocky brook or a wave-washed lake shore may not support any.

Managing the environment, as it is meant here, consists of working for combinations of land, food, water, and shelter and escape cover in ways that are favorable for the muskrats.

In many north-central marshes, the most important food for muskrats is the broad-leaved cattail. It thrives in shallow water and may almost disappear locally with protracted flooding. When water depths exceeding three to four feet in the central parts of marshes kill out extensive stands of cattails, the stands growing in the shallower parts of the same marshes may also die—I have been unable to learn exactly why from my botanist friends, but losses may be so severe that about the only broad-leaved cattails left alive are those becoming detached from the bottom to float in living clumps or mats on the surface of the water.

Once the cattail stands are gone from a flooded marsh, they are most likely to be restored through partial or complete exposure of the marsh bottom in late summer. The seeds then germinate in the mud, and, if the water does not come back so rapidly as to drown the seedlings, cattails may again be thriving in a year or two. Other important food plants of shallow marshes may decrease or increase as the water fluctuates. Prairie potholes that frequently go dry may have heavy fringing growths, not only of cattails but also of certain bulrushes and duck potatoes.

These patterns, however, are not invariable enough to justify too much generalizing. Although high water seldom is consistent with developing and maintaining the best of muskrat environments, it does not inevitably mean great shortage of muskrat food on a marsh or lake. Some bodies of water six feet or more in depth have an abundance of submerged plant life (especially pondweeds) that is suitable for muskrats.

On managed marshes having a controlled water supply, it may be possible to expose the bottoms of different parts of a marsh series in rotation, if that is needed to keep desirable plant life in good condition. A rotation schedule might leave only a small part of an area dry in any given year, yet permit the area as a whole to remain in a favorable state of productivity. Nor must the exposed parts necessarily lose all of their muskrats. Late summer, in addition to being the time when seeds of cattails and some other important food plants of muskrats germinate best, is the beginning of a period when muskrats are as little vulnerable to losses through warm-weather drought exposure as they ever are. If the muskrat manager is in a position to manipulate the water as he wishes, he might reflood some of the exposed bottom by fall—not too much to drown the cattail and bulrush seedlings but enough to improve the chances of the muskrats for taking care of themselves.

Hand planting of marsh plants may be practical on small areas when special circumstances justify the effort and expense. When this is done, it may be necessary to keep muskrats severely reduced for a year or so if they selectively cut the new plantings.

Management of wetlands for muskrats may require action against dominating vegetation of undesirable types. A great deal of work has been done on problems of aquatic weed control by fisheries biologists that is to some extent applicable to the problems of the muskrat manager—though it should be recognized that many of the plants considered undesirable in fish management are among the most desirable in muskrat management. The reader may get an idea of some measures that can be taken through consulting the paper by Speirs listed in the selected references.

Burning has been long employed to combat or to promote specific types of marsh vegetation. O'Neil's book describes it from the standpoint of muskrat management in Louisiana, emphasizing the role of the right kind of burning in the ecology of the Olney bulrush, the supremely important muskrat food of that region; and his statements undoubtedly have their application to other regions of Norh America. Marsh burning, if *carefully* done, can be useful in preventing destructive *uncontrolled* burning as well as to bring about changes in plant life.

For many years, the Wisconsin Conservation Department has studied ditching of shallow marshes as a means of improving environment for muskrats and other wildlife. Both the spoil banks and the water in the ditches have their advantages for muskrats and waterfowl, in particular. (See the selected reference on ditching by Mathiak and Linde.)

Some of the management techniques used on muskrat marshes are also applicable, with modifications, to streams. The deeper pools to be found in an intermittent stream have their own strategic values if located in food-rich places (as near corn fields), and dams or deflectors may be useful in maintaining them. Protection of desirable bank vegetation from grazing, burning, or clearing may be important and may fit in with soil conservation, stream improvement, and other good land-use practices. A short stretch of ordinary stock fencing may be all that is needed to safeguard a productive muskrat territory along a creek.

From what I have seen of the environmental manipulations for increasing muskrat production in north-central United States and south-central Canada, I would say that there are few rules of thumb that would always hold. The reader should therefore realistically understand that muskrat management may not only be a special field but a combination of special fields, much as is the practice of modern agriculture. Perhaps the problem is one of pollution or of fertility of waters. The occasional adverse effects of plant diseases, insect pests, or something unknown may have to be allowed for, along with the climatic unpredictables.

* * *

Tularemia and the hemorrhagic disease—sometimes operating together—*can* all but annihilate local muskrat populations and keep them reduced for years, sometimes on a regional scale. It is no exaggeration to say that hopes and plans for production of muskrat fur may have their uncertainties if not their futilities as long as the muskrat populations are swept by recurrent deadly epidemics.

The deadliest epidemics with which I have had experience have been traced to the hemorrhagic disease, and we have, by now, so many case histories of local epidemics that certain patterns have become well-defined. The reader who wishes may review the main features of epidemics back in Chapter IV, and the next few paragraphs are intended to help him recognize the hemorrhagic disease when he has specimens before him.

While examination of dead animals in a responsible manner may be advised as management routine, care should be taken to avoid touching possible infective material with bare hands and to avoid letting fluids from diseased animals soak through to clothing, table tops, etc. I use long-handled scalpels and forceps in my examinations, examine as many specimens as I can in the field (except when for good reason, specimens need to be brought inside), hold my face well away from the victims as I look through them, and use liberally the disinfectants recommended by the veterinary profession. One should remember that intestines full of gas can puff foully into one's face when punctured, that knives can slip while cutting through tough muskrat skin, and that even clean rubber gloves can become contaminated inside as well as outside if not properly used.

Identification of the visible lesions of the hemorrhagic disease is not always infallible, but some lesions are the more characteristic. (See again Figure 3.) Liver lesions may be in the form of small pus-like spots. Intestinal inflammation or hemorrhages can usually be recognized by observers who are familiar with the appearance of healthy intestines. There may be only a little bleeding here and there in the intestine, or the cecum (blind pouch) may be covered with purplish blotches, or the rectum may be full of blood. Lung hemorrhages of light or moderate intensity can be hard to distinguish from other types of congestion often occurring after death, but the more extreme cases (as when nearly a whole lobe has the appearance of a solid blood clot) are naturally less confusing. Bleeding from either mouth or anus, or from both, has been fairly indicative of hemorrhagic disease on the Iowa study areas, though it should not be assumed that lack of such bleeding proves that the victim did not die from the hemorrhagic disease.

The following suggestions for muskrat managers to keep down losses from the hemorrhagic disease may be taken up according to seasons of the year, starting with fall Harping on legalities again, I here assume that legal sanc tion exists or can be obtained for what needs to be done in efforts to control the disease.

Insofar as some of the worst epidemics on the Iowa study areas have been known to spread from small "hotspots," incipient epidemics should be discovered as early as possible. It would be well if someone cruised the more thickly populated parts of marshes and those with recent histories of disease losses, from early September to as late in the fall as traveling conditions permit. If muskrats are dying in accessible locations, the dead should be removed and the lodges dug up and leveled for a couple of hundred yards on all sides of the affected tracts. If the muskrats continue to die there, the digging into and leveling of the rebuilt lodges may be repeated, to see if that might slow down or stop the dying. The dead should be taken out of the water with paddles or poles and dropped into waterproof metal containers, taken to shore, and disposed of, preferably by burning.

Most diseased muskrats seem to die "at home" or to do no more than climb up on the side or top of a lodge and sit there—or they may sit off by themselves in some place like a coot nest—but, if they want to get away from their fellows, they can move substantial distances. When they do move from their familiar home ranges, they may travel either somewhat at random or along definite routes. Sometimes, a shoreline may become a highway for sick animals, in which case bodies of the diseased dead may be found both on land and in the water. The animals die in improvised nests, under hunters' boats, in holes up on the banks, and in channels of burrows and lodges. They die where muskrats are already dying or amid populations that previously had been suffering little or no loss from the disease.

In trying to reduce disease losses in winter, we may advantageously keep in mind the fact that, when northern marshes are ice-sealed and snow-covered, well-situated muskrats may seldom engage in surface activities—though, toward spring, some may become restless and come out on the thinning ice about the lodges. Also, when a freeze-out is in progress, all sorts of outside activities and "sign" of predation and scavenging may suggest no more than that the muskrats are in the trouble one might expect them to be in under the circumstances.

It is when the early winter or midwinter muskrat population appears to be secure and muskrats keep coming out *anyway* that we may have special reason to fear that an epidemic is getting under way.

Tip-offs afforded by the minks may be of the utmost value if their "sign" tends to be concentrated in certain parts of the marsh and especially in or near known "hot-spots." If there is a mink-bored clump of lodges having scattered muskrat remains and droppings containing musk-rat fur and bones outside of the mink holes, one might well cut open and look through sample lodges.

If evidence is found of muskrats dying in lodges or under the ice from a local epidemic, and if the approximate size of the area involved can be determined (here, again, the minks may show this), it may be well immediately to trap out the muskrats from and near the "hotspot." After that, it may be helpful to try to destroy the infectious lodges, as by burning or perhaps dynamiting. Or, as a less drastic measure, the chambers or nests where animals died might be opened up and treated chemically. Even cutting open the lodges and scattering the pieces should, I think, help to dilute sources of infection.

If I were a muskrat manager confronted by an incipient winter epidemic, I think that I should, to begin with, localize my trapping out and lodge destruction to within a radius of 50 yards of the lodges in which dying is known to be occurring. If the epidemic still continued to spread, operations might be extended to include the populations and lodges within a radius of as much as 200 to 300 yards. Perhaps the direction of the spreading fronts of the epidemic could be determined and the trapping and lodge destruction carried on in advance of them.

The sanitary measures advocated for the fall months apply, in general, to the spring months. It might be advisable to mark, as with wire stakes, the individual sites where dead animals are found on wet mud or in very shallow water, to treat these sites with disinfectants as the bottoms become exposed later in the summer—or, when feasible, saturate with disinfectants any places where diseased muskrats are found lying.

The usefulness of minks as indicators of disease mortality greatly diminishes after the coming of open water on the marsh. Yet, when minks do stay out in a marsh in spring to exploit the victims of local epidemics, their food habits can contribute important information. The food habits of minks ranging the shores may also reflect springtime epidemics in bank-dwelling muskrats.

The specimen material handled so far indicates that die-offs in early- and midsummer are all but characterized by the pneumonic form of the disease, the ways of which can be disconcertingly unpredictable. In late summer and early fall, the more ordinary types of the disease involving livers and intestines may show up more prominently, about the time that the previously vacant burrow systems in notorious "hotspots" are being rehabilitated by newcomer muskrats and when much general digging in the mud begins. This seasonal flaring, I suspect, may be initiated by renewed contacts of muskrats with the deadlier sources of infection.

Although minks continue to respond to availability of diseased dead muskrats in summer, much of the dying then occurs in places outside of regular travel routes of minks.

If otherwise inexplicably large quantities of muskrat remains are found in summer mink droppings, the possibility of disease are thereby indicated; but, if minks are not eating muskrats, no one should be too sure that disease losses may not be occurring.

Unless the problem of summer dying from disease becomes extraordinarily serious, I do not believe that I would recommend any large-scale leveling of lodges after the middle of May in north-central United States or after the end of that mouth in south-central Canada. These measures can be destructive of helpless young in the nests, and, at least at times, the net production of a marsh by fall becomes a matter of how many litters may be raised *despite* widespread and continuing disease losses.

In summer, as at other seasons, the chronic "hotspots" would seem to offer the best prospects for effective disease control. Here, the best management could well be to keep the "hotspot" areas in semi-permanent quarantine. Perhaps a small wet "hotspot" might be fenced around with chicken wire to prevent muskrats from living in it. Perhaps a "hotspot" exposed during dry weather might be worked over with a bulldozer or burned over with hot fires—used as a place for burning brush, old rubber, etc.? Perhaps judicious use of weed killers or repellents on favored food plants might discourage muskrats from using the most dangerous "hotspots." It could be good management to keep muskrats systematically trapped out of the deadliest parts of a marsh, even at times when their pelts had no value.

The importance of preventing, if possible, new "hotspots" from becoming established is evident from our case histories of epidemics. While I am now sure that at least some of the "hotspots" on the Iowa areas must have been infectious before my studies of epidemics began in 1943, certain marshes did seem to have been virtually free from the hemorrhagic disease in the first years following the drought exposures of the late Thirties and the early Forties. Most "hotspots" having traceable histories can be dated back to about the middle and late Forties and a few others to the early Fifties. These "hotspots" of convincingly recent origin were all places at which a little dying was recorded at first, then more and more, until their deadliness became quite regularly noted.

Management plans should take into account the evidence that the hemorrhagic disease, if not tularemia, too, occurs in most North American regions where there are muskrats. I do not think that any hopes for eradicating either disease are at all justifiable, and we had better learn to live with them.

Probably the best rule would be to avoid extremes. I think it would be risky management to try to winter concentrations of more than 20 muskrats per acre on first-class marshes even when close watch is kept for disease outbreaks, as the penalty for a mistake might be a thorough seeding of the marsh with contagion. My own preference would be for concentrations no greater than 10 per acre, or still fewer, if any real threat of disease exists on the marsh. And, in the spring, breeding densities greater than two pairs of adults per acre would seem to be undesirably high for the best of marshy environments.

* * *

Muskrats will doubtless continue to be taken by the million in the annual North American fur harvests, and we, as a public, will doubtless continue to consider them primarily as fur animals; but they need not be so regarded by everybody.

People may be interested in the animals merely for the sake of having them around, and these people have some rights as citizens along with the trappers and fur-buyers, and the rest. On private lands, people may make their own decisions as to what, if anything, to do about muskrats. On wildlife refuges, where the purpose of management may be to treat muskrats as members of complex natural communities, harvesting or human interference may not be called for.

If the purpose of protecting muskrats on an area is merely to spare them suffering incidental to fur trapping, I think that many of the arguments advanced can be unrealistic. From my own observations of the hemorrhagic disease, I would not say that ordinary steel-trap victims suffer any more than disease victims do, and I am sure that *good* drown-sets offer much the easier deaths for muskrats that do not want to die in any manner. We should consider also the chewed-up muskrats that hang about marsh edges or go blundering through areas full of hostile residents when population control of the species is entirely "natural." Unless the minks or foxes, etc., take care of them, they may live miserably for weeks. My intention is far from advocating trapping as an act of mercy—I wish but to put forth some facts that often seem to be completely lost sight of in arguments advanced against trapping.

If, however, the purpose of protecting muskrats on an area is to have opportunities to observe muskrats living like muskrats, for personal enjoyment or for serious study, then I can enthusiastically go along. If the purpose is to protect muskrats so we can watch them lying on quiet waters munching duckweeds or watch the wakes of swimmers or watch furry shapes sitting on ice or log or rush raft while they feed or dress, or to look at the lodges scattered over a marsh or at the "sign" along shore or at bubbles and food particles under clear ice, then that purpose makes sense to me. It makes sense to me if people want to know that muskrats live on a marsh where muskrats should live.

Muskrats rightfully belong in the North American out-of-doors as natives and as parts of certain types of landscapes that would be lacking without them.

CHAPTER VI

About Trappers and Especially Muskrat Trappers

TRAPPING FOR FUR may be a major economic support for entire regions in North America, not only in sparsely populated wildernesses and backwoods but also in the extensive marshy areas remaining in the midst of long-settled communities. Much trapping may be done about the ditches and streams of agricultural lands. The thousands of such places over the United States and southern Canada may collectively outyield the celebrated "fur countries" of the continent in annual proceeds from marketable raw furs. Even metropolitan areas may have "fur pockets," as of the muskrats and minks that live close to man as well as far away.

Fur trapping is but one form of human exploitation or harvesting of living resources. It is engaged in quite naturally by people having needs or inclinations to do so.

* * *

In northern "fur countries," trappers are not only of the public—they may just about *be* the public. Over some regions of central and northern Canada, trapping money represents almost all of the money (or the equivalents of money in goods) that many Indian or Eskimo families ever see. While part of the monetary income of people in other wilderness regions may come from guiding outsiders on hunting or fishing or traveling parties, from prospecting, or at times from doing something else besides trapping, the money from trapping still helps to pay for groceries, outboard motors, fancy dog harnesses, radios, and the whole run of manufactured necessities and luxuries of people living in remote areas. It is significant that the year-around "civilization" to be found very far away from railroads and other main travel routes in Canadian wildernesses so often consists of a Hudson's Bay Company post, possibly along with a church or an office of the Royal Canadian Mounted Police.

Of the Indian and Eskimo trappers of northern North America, the majority may be said to trap primarily because trapping is for them a customary fur-season occupation. Members of families or villages dependent upon a hunting economy go in for trapping as matter-of-factly as members of farming communities do their farming or as members of factory communities work in factories. These Indians and Eskimos vary in education and outlook from savages to literate, agreeable, and enlightened people; and, in physiques and personalities, from the chronically ailing and apathetic to superb athletes and people of courage and mature humor. About the same is true for the mixed breeds and the whites who have lived in the North for generations. They are all people, having their own assortments of racial or acquired traits.

There are also men of "civilized" backgrounds who become wilderness trappers from choice. They love the wilderness for its cleanness, freedom, beauty, and magnificent solitudes. I am never surprised, when in company with grown men, to hear, in effect: "You know what I'd like to do, someday? I'd like to take a few traps and spend a winter in the woods." Surely, there must be something fundamental in a wish so often expressed as practically to fall into a pattern—something fundamental in the power of the wilderness out-of-doors to draw and hold men who have alternative choices open to them.

Despite the intense love of nature that I have discovered beneath the taciturnity of several wilderness trappers I have come to know (including a "breed" with a high school education), I have never been able to satisfy myself as to how much wilderness trappers on the whole love either the wilderness or their lives as trappers. Certainly, they show little awareness of anything that can be labeled "romance of the fur trade" or show outward "THIS-IS-THE-LIFE" exultations. They may, in fact, show indifference toward outdoor beauty or, at an extreme, contempt for anyone fool enough to go into the wilderness without compelling cause—and a need to get away from artificial comforts hardly rates with them as a compelling cause! I have often thought that most of the wilderness trappers that I have known over the years (mainly whites but a considerable number of "breeds" and a few full-blooded Indians) would as willingly have done something else for a living—something easier—if given opportunities.

Some of the "born and bred" wilderness men may try "civilization" and give it up, even after going to college and enjoying personal successes, to return to their own people, their own environment, and their own old life. The trapping, itself, may exert no overwhelming attraction in these cases, except insofar as it is a wilderness vocation; but the most undemonstrative of natives may feel a sense of belonging where they are in the wilderness and in its hunting economies. This, together with loyalties toward friends and social units and the strength of traditional ways, may explain much of the psychology of especially the trappers of the Canadian North.

These northerners may or may not be much occupied with muskrat trapping, depending upon the region, the year, and the time of year. Where the muskrat abounds, as in the deltas of great northern rivers, it can be important to man, not only for its pelts but also as an excellent source of food.

*   *   *

It is in settled rather than wilderness regions that the muskrat is the staple fur-bearer; and, in settled regions, most trapping is done by youngsters before and after school hours, by farmers having time or finding time, and by the general public wishing and able to trap.

Individual school children have been known to earn as much in a month of trapping as their individual teachers earned in the same period. One farm boy caught over $200.00 worth of muskrats in a couple of weeks on a piece of land that originally cost his father less than that amount as a purchase price. A painter made enough during a week spent muskrat trapping to buy a refrigerator. A farmer bought a set of furniture with the profits of two trapping seasons from a fur-rich creek running through a 40-acre field. This farmer traps nearly every year, whether he makes any money at it or not, for the reason that he enjoys trapping. An elderly accountant has property on which he has managed to do some muskrat trapping each year for decades. In late years, he has not found it worth bothering about from the standpoint of fur returns, and he has been saying that each fur season is the last that he expects to trap, only to be back at it the next year. I think that he will continue to trap as long as he can get around.

These are among the trappers that may be called the amateurs—which is not to imply that they are dubbish, for at least some of them are expert trappers. As further examples may be mentioned a heating plant fireman, a carpenter, a restaurant owner, a state senator and his wife (both in their sixties), an electrician, an inventor and industrialist, and a farm grandmother whom I remember for her astuteness, courtesy, and good English.

These people are not far from a cross-section of the public liking outdoor pursuits—though I believe that it is more the case today than early in the century when I was young. Trapping then, as I remember it in South Dakota, was often considered proper for boys but something that they should normally outgrow when they reached manhood, with manhood's responsibilities for making money, developing the community, and occupying themselves with "serious" objectives.

It could be that the boys who trapped early in the century were more nearly a cross-section of at least rural and village boys than they are now. I can remember comparatively few boys of my own age in South Dakota who did not try fur trapping at some time, whereas not nearly such a large proportion of the boys of my present acquaintance in central Iowa have ever trapped.

One of the two chief motivations underlying "kid-trapping" is undoubtedly monetary. To children or teen-agers with limited earning power, the financial allurements of trapping may be strong—and the more unrealistic the hopes and expectations, the stronger it may be. Nor are price lists mailed out by fur companies always calculated to promote realistic thinking, as is to be perceived from the fantastic values often placed upon grades of furs that no one seems ever to get.

The second motivation is what may be called the Daniel Boone or Davy Crockett heritage, the residual glamour of the backwoodsman or plainsman or voyageur in North American tradition. Another motivation *may* be enjoyment of the out-of-doors, with trapping as a pass-key; but, as a parent and a friend of parents, I am unwilling to try to appraise the strength of outdoor esthetics in the very young.

But, let there be no question about it, Iowa boys (and some girls) still comprise thousands of the fur trappers in that anything-but-frontier state, especially those living in places where trapping may be conveniently carried on close to home, as on the farm. It is true that some youngsters soon become discouraged by the unimpressive returns from their trapping efforts and give up. Or they find their trapping terminated by family edict—as after catching their first skunk. Other youngsters catch enough for variable amounts of spending money and continue trapping each fur season until they leave home. A few follow trapping as a hobby or livelihood in their later years.

Every North American community having exploitable fur resources seems to have some professional or semi-professional fur trappers. These men are to be distinguished from year-around trappers hired by public agencies to keep down depredations of predatory animals upon livestock in that they take animals during the months when raw furs are marketable and try to operate on a basis of sustained fur yields, year after year. They may devote most or all of their working time to trapping for periods of a week or two up to three or more months each year.

Young men or old, those who make a business of fur trapping are usually people of extraordinary physical stamina and ability to withstand hardship if need be, and their trapping may be characterized by hard work while it lasts. They are farmers, skilled or unskilled laborers, salaried employees, or persons in almost any vocation who either take time off for the trapping or try to do their regular work and trapping, too. The latter combination *can* be rated as a rugged undertaking for those who work at jobs during the day and do their trapping at night, or vice versa, and somehow try to sleep in between.

Professional or semi-professional trapping in an agricultural state such as Iowa may be of modest scope or otherwise. Someone has permission to trap on a number of farms near home. Someone else traps public-owned roadways (strategic trap sites frequently being found under bridges), covering considerable distances daily by motor car. Others trap competitively on public-owned lakes and marshes, though informal agreements between trappers may serve to eliminate frictions and to establish something akin to trapping rights. The owner of an exceptionally good fur marsh may find it profitable to trap full time during the trapping season or to hire trappers or to lease the trapping rights for cash or shares. On the larger private marshes of duck shooting clubs and "rat ranches," the fur trapping may all be done by hired professionals or under contract. Trapping on many major fur areas under public ownership may be restricted to permit-holders making up a virtually professional group.

Prospects for money-making certainly provide motivation for fur trapping by adult persons. The most profitable trapping of which I have known in Iowa yielded about $4,000.00 in muskrat and mink pelts to a man—aided by his wife—in no more than six weeks, and this man had no more wonderful fur resources to draw from than had his fellow citizens. He knew just what he was doing and worked hard at it. Few others, even of experienced and well-situated professionals, may expect such rich fur harvests, but it is not unusual for expert trappers to catch between $500.00 and $1,000.00 worth of fur during their better trapping seasons.

The inflation of raw fur prices that took place after the first World War furnished an example of what profit motivation may be. Prior to 1919, I remember selling muskrat pelts for from a few cents to around 50¢ each. Then, in the winter of 1919-20, the price for muskrat pelts approached $3.00 flat rate in my neighborhood—and got up to $5.00 averages in Canada. In that winter, the South Dakota countryside had an influx of mechanics, clerks, laborers, and the general unemployed from towns, many completely inexperienced in trapping and poorly equipped, setting traps wherever they could. There were disappointments, trap and fur thefts, arguments, fist fights, and the disagreeable by-products of human grabbiness made more disagreeable by what were considered prospects for quick and easy money.

But nothing that looks much like easy money can be seen in the trapping prospects during many years, and still the "regulars" come out with their traps. One of the "regulars"—whose "civilized" vocation requires a high degree of skill and pays accordingly—is out trapping on a public marsh during every fur season. So far as I know, he always loses money at it and sometimes more than he says he can afford. There are numerous farmers and townspeople, alike, who maintain that they seldom expect to do more than break even, economically, on the trapping, yet, each year, feel that they must take their fling at it.

*   *   *

Nostalgia is behind much of the trapping done by grown men. For many who were "kid trappers"—and so many were—a brief return to trapping once a year enables them to relive, a little bit, some of their youth and the things about youth that seem so precious after they are lost. A man may be perfectly realistic in knowing that he is not young again but still enjoy the trapping (or hunting or fishing) that he did when he was young simply because of his earlier enjoyments. To a certain extent, a reversion to trapping (as to hunting or fishing) partakes of the ritualistic. With the coming of brisk fall weather, with wood smoke in the air from old-fashioned farm house chimneys, with the new track "sign" and digging of burrows and building of muskrat lodges in the wet places, those of us who are susceptible to old thought patterns start thinking . . . .

Love of the out-of-doors, exactly that, is surely among the non-monetary motivations behind fur trapping by the "regulars." This is not to contend that all trappers always love the out-of-doors nor that any trappers ever love it more than they do. Anyone should realize that trappers, being human, at times feel something less than satisfaction in their surroundings, in accepting the hardships and uncertainties that can be a part of trapping.

Love of the out-of-doors may be a passion so acute that it truly hurts, whether elicited by the out-of-doors rather generally or only by particular aspects of the out-of-doors. Or, it may be an indefinite feeling, manifested by a sense of rightness or of peace. A person receptive toward solitude may find in it a priceless quality, not only when the solitude is combined with beautiful panoramas but also with very local outdoor beauty. All who love deserts, mountains, forests, tundras, marshes, the sea, the vastnesses of the upper air and outer space must be familiar with this quality to some degree.

We need not make unrealistic assumptions here either, for it does not follow that those who can love solitude must want it without interruption, always. I have seen many times, both in the North Woods and in the out-of-the-way West, the welcome given a friendly visitor by someone reputed to be a recluse, the bringing out of canned delicacies hoarded for a special event, the urging to stay over-night and so on. But no one should underestimate the blessing that solitude can be for people in need of it.

Love of the wild animals that one preys upon is not at all incompatible with trapping or hunting or fishing. It is something that I have experienced personally from childhood throughout my life. The psychology of outdoorsmen in this respect, however, is not always easy to analyze from their talk and actions concerning this animal or that, and I shall not maintain that it is free from inconsistencies.

Challenges in the tasks to be accomplished and pride

in feats of ability may be decidedly among the motivations of expert trappers continuing their trapping. To some people, the taking of enormous fur catches with the aid of hired help, extensive leasing, aircraft transportation, etc., amounts to "big business," and, as such, has its appeal, even when the chances of monetary profits actually are slight. Someone else takes pride in lesser jobs skillfully done, such as a farmer in catching more fur along his creek than anyone else believed to be in the neighborhood. Although I would not say how much the best of trappers enjoy trapping under extremely difficult weather conditions, those making fair catches in weather so bad as to force the other trappers to quit are not lacking in their own sources of gratification.

Then, there is a kind of companionship to be found among at least some trappers, including those trapping in competition on the muskrat marshes. A trapper coming in wet, cold, tired, hungry, and lonesome to his own camp is invited over to another's camp, where someone has a warm meal ready, where he may thaw out, eat, rest, and talk before returning to his own chores at his own camp. Perhaps someone "just drops in" at another's camp, to sit around for an hour or so. The gossip may be about anything about which people talk—or the visitor may ask if someone wants something brought out from town in the morning. This is nothing that does not have equivalents in many other places, but trapping camps are among the places where friendships begin and thrive over the years.

One more attraction of trapping for civilized men, especially for those who must spend much of their lives indoors: Along with gardening, hiking, hunting, fishing, golfing, and almost any outdoor activity, trapping may be one of the healthful things that people do. Short of what would be physical excess for one's age or state of health, it can be one of the best of body-builders, with its walking, chopping, rowing or paddling, carrying, lifting, bending over, dragging of sleds or toboggans, skiing or snowshoeing, with its hours in the open air. When one of its returns is tranquillity of mind, its health-giving possibilities are immeasurably increased. In its very strenuous types, it is more of a "young man's game" than one for the middle-aged, or older, but the older people need not be out of it if possessed of ordinarily sound physiques and good judgment. It may offer an enjoyable and wholesome hobby, a partial antidote for some of the evils of high-pressure, artificialized living.

At any rate, we have people who are trappers, young ones and old ones, and people becoming trappers, city people among them. Others do what they can to put cherished daydreams into substance, if it be no more than to walk along the nearest stream or lake shore or to subscribe to a trappers' magazine.

* * *

Fur trapping, of muskrats or of other fur-bearers, may be expected to have its modernizations as a part of modern life. By this, I do not mean modernization in the sense of motor transportation or gadgetry. Modernity also works toward reduction or elimination of the worst drawbacks of old-fashioned trapping. Increased enlightenment is reflected in many trapping regulations. Registered trapline systems are introducing long-needed reforms into wilderness trapping, and certain of their benefits may be extended to other kinds of trapping. Trappers' associations that are well administered can and do promote fair dealing among the trappers and in the fur trade, as well as improved methods in the harvest and management of fur-bearers. The areas now managed carefully for fur production include many of the best fur areas on our continent, and this trend should continue.

CHAPTER VII

Trapping Muskrats in Open Water

IN OUR NORTH-CENTRAL region, muskrat pelts are unlikely to reach a desirable stage of primeness or marketable quality before about the first of December, which usually means a couple of weeks or so after freeze-up. However, the trappers representing the general public may prefer to do their harvesting of the annual muskrat crop before freeze-up. Then is the time of easy, large-scale harvesting—that is, as long as the weather and the water levels remain favorable.

The sets made in ice-free water at the base of landings have a distinct appeal for almost all muskrat trappers, from novices to professionals. On the right kind of late-fall day or night, when abundant muskrats are active and waters are quiet and traps are set where and how they should be set, the muskrats may be caught by the hundreds or thousands, even on a local scale. With three or four or a week of such days in succession, the season's muskrat trapping may be about finished over most of a state like Iowa. It may be easy trapping, as trapping goes. In fact, the relative ease of fall trapping of muskrats may be so great as to outweigh other considerations in the minds of the trapping public as long as passable prices may be received for the fall-trapped pelts.

From the standpoint of muskrat management, fall trapping has its advantages at some times and places. In some areas where muskrat trapping in winter or spring is standard procedure, so-called salvage trapping is carried on in the fall. The purpose of salvage trapping is to remove the animals that are in a bad way because of drought exposure, food shortage, overpopulation, or some other natural crises. Not only may it be economically advantageous to make some use of the animals that would stand little chance of surviving the coming winter, but it may also be good management to eliminate restless and quarrelsome parts of populations so that they may not cause trouble for the rest of the muskrats in the neighborhood. Also, when sweeping disease losses threaten a heavy muskrat population before winter begins, the urgent need may be to take out a lot of muskrats, whether their pelts are worth much or not.

The main talking point in favor of spring trapping, in open water after the ice has gone out, is that the pelts of the muskrats are in "full prime" only in spring. Technically, this is true. Actually, many fur-buyers prefer winter-caught muskrat pelts for most commercial uses, and the time naturally comes in the spring when the fur loses value because of shedding, wear, bleaching, etc.

And large numbers of spring muskrat pelts may be seriously damaged, if not ruined, by fight wounds. Biological surpluses or social misfits among the muskrats may get into (and cause) more and more trouble with the advance of the breeding season. When a quarter of the spring-caught muskrat pelts are classed as "damaged" by the buyers (and docked accordingly), the economic advantages of postponing the muskrat harvest until pelts are in technical full prime become hard to see.

My main objections to open-water spring trapping in the north-central region are to its wasteful possibilities in still other respects. This kind of trapping can be especially destructive to migrating waterfowl heading northward, mated, toward their breeding grounds. Furthermore, wintering of heavy populations of muskrats *may* entail the well-known risks from disease or winter-killing. Sometimes, all goes well and nearly as many muskrats are present in the spring as were present in the preceding fall, but, in view of what can happen in several months between freeze-up and break-up, I would not suggest counting on anything too confidently. The hemorrhagic disease, alone, may confound arguments as to the advantages of spring trapping. So may, on occasion, an obstinately sinking frost line.

Let us say that our muskrat trapping is to be done at times of open water, either in fall or in spring. Such may be the time specified by law, or the customary time for trapping in an area, or the time when trapping must be done in order to compete with one's fellow-trappers, or, for any other reason, the time when one traps muskrats. What, then, are some good methods?

* * *

In fall trapping, the trapper has a special advantage in that the muskrats are *busy* and return repeatedly to "key" sites of activity. They build and remodel lodges and feed houses and sitting places of vegetation out in or at the edge of the water. They make trails from water's edge to shore or up on the lodges. They show favoritism for certain places.

Where muskrats are abundant and active, there may be hardly a place in which a functional set trap might not catch a muskrat, sooner or later. Nevertheless, the difference between good and poor trapping techniques is in part a matter of selecting the sort of trap sites that any normal muskrat just cannot stay away from. It is neither a necessary nor a desirable harvesting technique to scatter large numbers of traps around, almost everywhere. In suitable open-water trapping weather and by means of possibly 50 to 100 traps set at well-chosen sites, a trapper should be

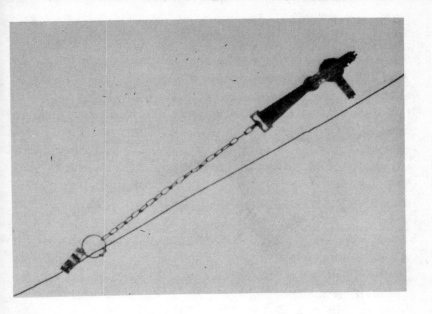

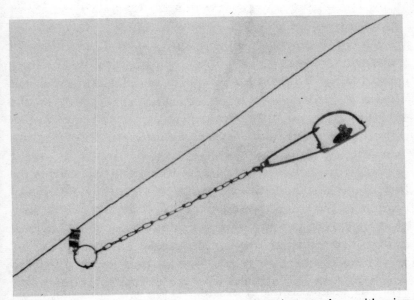

FIGURE 12. "Among the devices to promote drowning are those with wires . . . permitting movement in one direction but no return." Photos by Iowa State College Photoservice.

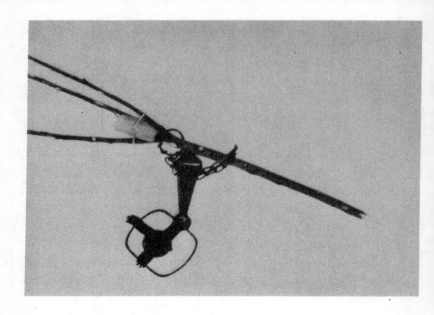

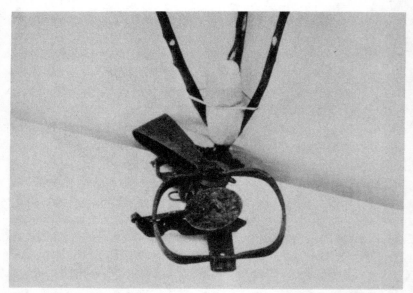

FIGURE 13. Under-water bait set for muskrats living in food-poor environment. Upper shows trap, bait, and stake ready for setting under the ice; lower shows depth to which stake should be pushed in sand or mud bottom and position of bait in relation to trap. Photos by Iowa State College Photoservice.

able to take, in a few days, all of the muskrats that should be taken from a fair-sized tract of north-central marsh.

In this kind of trapping, two or three traps set at the edge of each of the larger regularly used lodges and single traps at the more inviting of the smaller lodges and sitting places should be enough. One should refrain from setting at places where victims are unlikely to drown if a few almost certain drown sets can be made for the same muskrats in the same vicinity. When, by judicious setting, one catches nearly a muskrat per trap per day in six traps per acre and, let us say, some eight to 12 muskrats per acre represent the harvestable part of the population, one can afford to be choosy as to trap sites as long as competition with other trappers leaves any choice.

Some sites are naturally very attractive and others can be built up or remodeled to attract muskrats to them. If it is illegal to set traps at the bases of lodges, or if the muskrats live in the banks of bodies of water having few if any lodges and do much swimming in open water, artificial floats anchored in strategic places may have big possibilities. At any rate, it is usually not difficult to find or to improvise places that the muskrats come to if they come in the neighborhood at all. This requires that the trapper have only an elementary ability to read the "sign" represented by droppings, food remains, cuttings, pathways, and building activities of the muskrats, as well as some knowledge of muskrat behavior.

Once the general trap sites are chosen that the muskrats will be almost certain to visit during their periods of outside activity, the trapper should try to reduce the element of luck in getting the animals into the traps. If the traps are merely set somewhere about the bases of lodges or on fairly large surfaces of rush rafts or feeding beds, visiting muskrats may or may not get into them. I remember seeing, at several different times during a day, one or more muskrats climbing up and feeding and moving around over about two square feet of the flattened base of a small lodge without getting into a trap known to be set under water at the edge. To set traps right, one should take advantage of muskrat psychology.

The most effective open-water fall trapping that we carried on in connection with the Iowa experiments put a muskrat in practically every trap during each night that muskrats were there to get into them. Such effectiveness depended not only upon proper attention to the over-all features of the trap sites but also upon exploitation of the tendency of muskrats to swim or climb *between* floating or elevated material at landings.

This means inducing the animal to land precisely where the trap awaits. In practice, one may scoop away material at the water's edge at the base of the landing on the side of a lodge and heap this material along the sides of the landing in such a way as to leave a little channel with shoulders, both to receive the trap and to guide the muskrat into it. One may, when setting traps around the edge of a large lodge, make a suitable bed for a trap by leveling the material slightly below the surface of the water (or, if necessary, building an even, firm foundation) and then heaping up more vegetation off to the side of the lodge. The trap should lie between the lodge and the new heap of vegetation protruding from the water (Figure 7). When the trap site is on a small floating raft of vegetation, the central part may be depressed and the rest heaped up on both sides, to leave a wet valley connected with the surrounding water for the trap. I do not wish to make overly broad assertions, but I doubt if any normal north-central muskrat engaged in normal fall activities can long keep away from a trap in one of these "invitational" sets if the muskrat comes near it.

Another point should be considered, especially in using artificial floats as trap sites. If the floats offer the muskrats sitting places in water in which sitting places are scarce, and in which the muskrats do much swimming back and forth, float sets *can* be most effective. If, however, floats are put here and there in a thickly vegetated marsh having dozens of alternative sitting places occurring naturally, they may not be worth the work of putting them out and the traps committed to them. When float sets are used, they should be so constructed to permit heaping with vegetation and setting traps in ways to afford the nearest equivalent of the "invitational" sets that work best around the muskrat's own constructions.

Marsh-dwelling muskrats in our region may not often go to land during the fall of the year unless something is wrong. Mud lodges and land trails may be prominent during falls when drought conditions prevail. At times of acute shortages of cattails, bulrushes, and other good natural foods out in a marsh, muskrats may be forced ashore. Seldom have I seen foraging by muskrats in corn fields planted near the larger marshes, but, when this does occur, it may be conspicuous. Shore activities that are thus concentrated in certain places afford variable numbers of suitable trap sites, but I would not advise setting traps in the trails or at shallow water landings if the same muskrats are readily to be caught in deeper-water drown sets. Baits, such as ears of corn in areas where marsh muskrats have learned to recognize and to relish corn, may be tried if baits seem to be needed—though, as a rule, I doubt that baiting with food has special usefulness in most trapping of muskrats on north-central marshes.

Traps covered by water are usually sufficiently concealed for trapping north-central muskrats. Rarely, an individual muskrat "specializes" in heaping vegetation on traps. During one of the Iowa trapping experiments, six out of the recorded seven trap burials occurred at one place and undoubtedly represented the activities of a single muskrat. There were burials at this one place on each of the four nights of the experiment. This burying appeared to be purposeful, though most of the incidents of traps being buried or plugged with debris that trappers notice are probably accidental. The buried traps may simply be in the way of muskrats building or repairing lodges and are buried because a muskrat happens to carry or drag wadded vegetation over the trap.

Traps should be placed where they will not likely be knocked over or pushed off and where their action will be unimpeded by heavy stems or roots. A trapper may not always be successful in protecting traps from wave action or drifting debris, but he can keep in mind the possibilities and remove by hand the coarser floating material that might drift or be pushed into traps by swimming muskrats.

The traps should also be arranged, with respect to the probable direction of approach of the muskrat, so as to reduce the chances of the action of springs, jaws, or triggers knocking feet out of the way. In practice, this means turning the springs of long-spring traps off toward the trigger side (both to get the springs partly out of the way of feet and to allow the free jaws to lie flatter) and then placing the traps in the channels or trails, lengthwise to the action of the jaws. Springs should lie in the opposite direction from the probable approach. The direction of probable approach to traps at the side of a lodge is from the water, but, where muskrats swim along past the edge of a lodge, they may come in from either side. Then, traps should merely be placed with jaws closing lengthwise to lines of travel and in whatever ways they lie most securely and flat. The more compact jump traps may be easier to set in some places, but they have their own disadvantages. Most muskrat trappers I know prefer traps of long-spring design.

Much of my personal enthusiasm for the "stop-loss" traps is due to the relative ease with which they, when used for muskrats, are placed in an effective position. With common steel traps, a good trapper must try to catch as many as he can of the animals by their strong hind legs rather than by their weak forelegs. This is not always easy to do, nor can it always be done with regularity. With "stop-losses," catching by forelegs need not be avoided. I think that, with "stop-losses," it is not only easier but preferable to catch muskrats by forelegs. About all that most such victims can do when caught in "stop-losses" is to wriggle backward, and, if there is sufficient water for drowning anywhere within their reach, they stand a good chance of drowning in it (Figure 9).

Muskrats are often held better when caught by hind legs in "stop-losses" than in common steel traps, but, for such holds, the advantages of the "stop-losses" over the common steel traps are not as pronounced as when the catches are by the forelegs—except when the animals are precariously held, as by single toes. One-toe grips almost never hold a muskrat in the jaws of a common steel trap if the animal is in a position to struggle, but in "stop-losses" they— notably hind-toe grips—may be about as effective as the more secure grips, even when the victims remain alive (Figure 10).

I am not sure that capture by a hind leg in a "stop-loss" insures drowning more promptly than would the same kind of hold in a common steel trap of equal weight, but the added incumbrance of the "stop-loss" guard to a trapped muskrat probably does work toward this end, despite the freedom of movement still permitted by a hind leg grip.

A trapper placing a common steel trap in such a way as to increase the chances of a muskrat being caught by a hind foot while climbing out of the water must try (1) to have the muskrat swim or lift its forefeet over the trap and (2) then have it walk into the trap with hind feet. This calls for discrimination to be done right. The best rule of which I know is to deepen the bottom of the landing just below the water's edge, so that the trap can be placed three or four inches below the surface and as close as possible to the landing where the muskrat climbs out. Some trappers try for the same results by placing traps on the natural slope of the lodge with the spring pointing downward at an angle of about 30 degrees and the trap pan some three or four inches beneath the surface, but I have seen enough of these traps dislodged or passed by swimming muskrats to question any advantages of the method over preparing a suitable place for the trap closer to the landing.

Drowning of muskrats caught in common steel traps may be facilitated in several ways. Some trappers use No. 1½ sizes instead of the usual No. 1 for muskrats, not only to gain a higher grip on the legs (which does not always happen) but also for the advantage the greater weight may have for drowning. (A No. 1 trap may, of course, be artificially weighted.) Then, there are tricks in fastening the traps for drowning, of which the simplest is merely putting the trap stake in deep water, as far out from the trap-set at the landing as the chain permits. The placing of an extra stake in deep water six to 10 inches from the stake that holds the trap gives the victim something about which to entangle the chain and thus be prevented from returning to shallow water.

The standard stakes used by professional trappers on Iowa muskrat marshes are of small to medium sizes of bamboo poles, usually with identifying cloth streamers tied to the tops. For the sake of economy or convenience, willow or other hardwood poles of suitable thickness, length, and strength may be used, especially when sufficiently dead and dry as not to be attractive food items for the muskrats. Whatever kind of non-metal stake is used, not only should it be put through the ring of the trap chain but the ring (or an adjacent link) should also be firmly wired to the stake in such a manner that it cannot come loose in the event of the stake being cut off by a muskrat at or above the surface of the water. Sometimes, a trapped animal that does not promptly drown chews up a stake. Sometimes, a perfectly free and uninjured and comfortable one does the same. Perhaps this is for no apparent reason other than the animal wishes to gnaw. Perhaps, the animal incorporates the pieces of the stake into the lodge, along with cattail and bulrush stems. Whatever happens, a trapper should always guard against victims escaping with traps attached.

While well-set common steel traps may drown nearly all of the muskrats caught in them, provided that the water is sufficiently deep, drowning in these does not always occur promptly. A considerable period of swimming back and forth may elapse before the victim—especially a large one —tires and drowns. With the greater restriction of movement imposed by the "stop-loss" traps, drowning rates speed up decidedly for at least the animals caught by forelegs. It is, however, in shallow water trapping that the "stop-losses" show up so advantageously.

One of the Iowa trapping experiments was conducted on a marsh having large tracts that were drought-exposed or covered by very shallow water. No more than 58 traps— including 12 of "stop-loss" design—were set at one time. Complete "runs" of the traps were made once or twice each 24 hours. The eight "runs" that were made in a five-day period yielded 272 muskrats, with catches diminishing to 23 on the final "run." In taking these 272, 13 were recorded as having escaped by "wringing," and these 13 were practically all animals caught in very shallow water by common steel traps. When the "stop-losses" were substituted for common steel traps in the shallows, the losses from "wring-offs" all but ceased. The victims of these modern traps drowned in no more than three to five inches of water in the majority of cases.

The site of another trapping experiment was a marsh so nearly dry that common steel traps could not have been used without excessively high rates of loss and mangling. Two dozen "stop-loss" traps (12 each of the two commercial makes that were conveniently available) were given four morning "runs." Counting two muskrats taken between "runs," 71 muskrats were taken from the 24 traps in the four mornings, with the catches for the last two mornings having dropped to 15 and 14, respectively, as the trapping thinned down the population on the tracts of marsh covered. In trapping those 71 muskrats—usually in water from three to six inches deep and averaging about four inches—only one animal escaped after having been caught and that one left only a front toe between the trap jaws. Eight of the animals were successfully held by single hind toes; two, by two hind toes; and two, by two front toes. Only two had mangled legs, and one of these animals had drowned quickly after getting into the trap. Seventeen were alive at times when the "runs" were made, mostly animals held by unmutilated hind toes. Common steel traps set under similar conditions probably would have lost through "wring-offs" half to three-quarters of the muskrats getting into them, and most of those held probably would have been badly mangled and alive in the traps when found.

These experimental results illustrate a distinction to be again emphasized. Although the "stop-losses" are steel traps, their use *can* represent progress toward humane as well as efficient harvesting of muskrats as a fur crop.

*   *   *

Stream trapping of muskrats before freeze-up may be

either easy or difficult, depending upon circumstances. It is the one type of muskrat trapping that most Iowans are in a position to do, and one of the main reasons for the usual opening of our trapping season for muskrats on November 10, before the muskrats' schedule of pelt-priming is as far advanced as it should be to give a quality product. In short, the Iowa general public, including farm youngsters, traps its muskrats before freeze-up or it usually does not trap them at all.

As in open-water fall trapping on marshes, traps are set at the bases of landings for muskrats in stream habitats. Here the usual landings are at the edge of muddy or sandy banks or bars, where the animals either sit or travel along land trails to cornfields, orchards, or to other attractions awaiting them away from the stream. They may do much foraging on the stream banks or in bordering fields, or they may hardly leave the water's edge. In either case, their landing places are typically recognizable and suitable for trap sites.

Fluctuating water levels may be a major source of difficulty in stream trapping. The relation of surface water to the traps may be about right for a few days, or perhaps gradual lowering of the water calls for resetting traps in beds a little lower down; then rains come, and the water rises far over the traps. If trapping is attempted during the time between open water and freeze-up, when ice forms and melts again, or just lines the shores or seals the surfaces in the eddies, the problems of making good sets and keeping them workable are increased.

Floats may be useful as trap sites in streams during periods of fluctuating water levels—assuming that the muskrats are inclined to use them. The muskrats do not invariably respond to the floats that trappers put out for them, and, as long as the muskrats are independent animals, doing about as they please, this is quite to be expected.

Baits, too, may be useful in stream trapping—assuming again that the muskrats are attracted to them. The muskrats do not have to respond to baits, either, if they do not feel like it. Carrots and apples probably have as much intrinsic appeal to muskrat appetites as anything commonly used as baits. Even marsh muskrats having access to an abundance of favorite natural foods may be observed responding to carrots or apples, at least on occasion. If the local population of muskrats has already discovered the delights of a cornfield, ear corn may be excellent bait, but this presupposes some degree of "education" on the part of the muskrats. If ear corn is offered to muskrats that do not know what it is—and this may be true of extensive populations, in corn belt environments as well as elsewhere—corn-baited traps may be ineffective.

On the whole, the best kind of attraction for muskrats in open-water stream trapping is not bait at all. It is simply the kind of place that invites swimming muskrats to climb on, and the muskrats often clearly indicate their preferences for such places by the "sign" they leave.

Trappers use many types of drown sets for muskrats in shallow ditches and natural streams. Some lengthen trap chains (extension chains are on the market) and put stakes for entangling out toward the center of a small stream. Among the devices used to promote drowning are those with wires or stakes permitting movement in one direction but no return (Figure 12). A skillful trapper thus guides a victim to almost any place within reach where he wishes it to drown, including places under overhanging banks or near the bottoms of pools or otherwise offering more or less concealment from the eyes of scavengers or even of possible human snoopers. When common steel traps are used, the desirability of catching muskrats by hind legs is still greater in shallow stream trapping than in ordinary marsh trapping. A trapper may increase the chances for hindleg catches along streams in much the same way as on marshes, by modifying the base of the landing and setting the trap in close to the landing and too deep in the water for a swimming muskrat to reach with forefeet.

In late years, the greater abundance of raccoons and beavers about north-central water courses has increased the necessity for *securely* fastening the chains of traps set in the water for muskrats. Whether one also tries to catch these larger animals or not, no one wants them to get away with muskrat traps on feet—a matter to be considered both in selecting trap sites and in making the sets. A solidly anchored small trap may permit a large-footed, powerful animal to pull out or may hold it by a couple of toes so that it can be released with slight injuries if the trapper, for legal or other reasons, wishes to release it.

* * *

Open-water spring trapping of muskrats in the north-central region has fewer features in common with open-water fall trapping than might often be expected. One still selects as trap sites the landings favored by swimming muskrats, but many of the types of sets that were most useful in the open water of fall may not continue to be so effective in the open water of spring. Only an occasional muskrat may climb up on the sides of the main dwelling lodges during the open-water period immediately following break-up. Spring may not be a time of any notable construction work on the part of the muskrats until quite late in the season, when the females are repairing or building lodges for the housing of their young and when fur trapping should no longer be done, anyway.

Carry-overs in winter behavior of the muskrats are responsible for some of the difficulties of open water spring trapping. At any season, a muskrat leaves its dwelling lodge by diving from the inner chamber into a plunge hole, unless, for some reason, it has a passageway over the water leading directly through the side of the lodge from the chamber to the outside. When out in the open water away from the lodge, it climbs or tries to climb on whatever floating or protruding objects it wants to, in spring and in fall, alike. But, in spring when returning to the lodge, the swimmer seems far more apt to dive, to enter the outer opening of the plunge hole, and to come up in the chamber—much as it had been doing while swimming under the ice all winter. Thus, in spring, there is no uniformly compelling attraction about the sort of "invitational" set at the base of an occupied lodge that works so well in the fall.

More difficulties in spring trapping may result from the absence of *strategic* landings in the vicinities of even well-used main lodges—with muskrats having large numbers of landings or sitting places differing little in attractiveness. Yes, traps set all over may be expected to catch some muskrats, but a trapper accustomed to 75% to 90% averages in fall trapping may see a difference the first time he tries spring trapping in, for example, a dense stand of cattails.

Add the fact that many of the floats, rush rafts, or lodge butts lying well out in marshy open spaces and furnishing the muskrats with strategic places to sit are likewise strategic places for the ducks to sit, and we have the repertoire of a conscientious spring trapper cut down still more

Nevertheless, by reading what the muskrats reveal through their "sign," the spring trapper can usually find many good and legitimate trap sites in certain tracts of marsh—open-topped nests, habitually used lodge butts, and those landings at the bases of lodges that the musk rats plainly *are* using. Some of these places may be so scented with muskrat musk that even humans with their dull sense of smell have no difficulty recognizing that muskrats come to them. Some trappers bait with muskrat musk, but I can not make up my mind as to how effective this is.

Lines of travel of dispersing or wandering muskrats along lake or marsh shores or stream banks may also be trapped, but fight wounds may reduce the marketability of the animals so taken. The proportion of damaged pelts among the transients becomes greater as transients consist more and more of chronic wanderers. Still, the muskrats dispersing from wintering quarters may be relatively wound-free. When movements are heavy along those streams serving as regular travel routes, expert trappers catch hundreds in a week or so, before the serious fighting starts. This kind of trapping becomes mainly a matter of taking advantage of the natural landings that muskrats, resident or transient, may be depended upon to visit.

Flood waters may be no help in harvesting a muskrat crop by means of traps unless the animals congregate more on anchored floats. The muskrats that I have observed during spring floods sat around on anything from tree trunks and lodged debris to perches in willow thickets and on the land bordering the high water. (See again Figure 1.) The more the waters recede within the stream banks, the easier it generally becomes to find trap sites on sand bar points or bases of cut banks or trails leading up on shore. At the lower and steadier water stages, spring trapping of muskrats more nearly resembles fall trapping in stream habitats.

* * *

Open-water harvesting of muskrats may not require the use of steel traps, everywhere, but steel traps (including "stop-losses") are almost everywhere standard and lawful equipment.

Other devices reflect much human ingenuity. Wire mesh funnel traps or cage traps are set at burrow or lodge entrances. Kegs with open tops are anchored down in water in such a way that muskrats climb over the rim and get in without being able to get out. Or there are boxes with trap-door covers. Or something else may be put out with the idea of catching many muskrats quickly and easily.

Anyone interested in trying out harvesting methods not using steel traps should first make sure of the legality of what he proposes to do. I can not help feeling doubtful that the majority of experienced trappers would care to switch over from steel traps to the other methods of which I know even if the latter were legal and effective. A trapper who finds his few dozen "stop-losses" filled with drowned muskrats on each "run" as long as muskrats remain to get into them may not see the need for going to much work or expense in trying something new unless the new method should offer truly special promise.

Shooting with a .22 caliber rifle is one of the methods of harvesting muskrats in wilderness areas of northern North America after the ice goes out in the spring, and it is easy to see how such shooting has advantages under particular circumstances. In settled communities, shooting of rifles over water has its possibilities of injury to man or livestock from glancing bullets and may be prohibited by law. Shooting of muskrats with a shotgun is so damaging to fur values as to be unjustifiable in fur-harvesting (as distinguished from pest control) even if legally permissible.

Shooting, too, must be well done if it is to be an effective and humane method of harvesting muskrats. Wounded muskrats escape, perhaps to die, the same as other wounded animals, and only a few parts of a muskrat's body are so vital that bullets striking them bring instant death. Mortally wounded muskrats may still have aptitudes for diving and getting under something before completely losing control of their actions. A bullet placed at the base of the brain almost always kills in a satisfactory manner, but it is not always easy to place a bullet at the base of the brain, or at any other selected spot, especially at a considerable distance when shooting off hand or from a not-completely-steady boat or canoe.

Furthermore, opportunities for shooting muskrats vary with environment, weather, time of year, wariness of the animals, and so on. In actuality, north-central trappers seldom have many good chances to shoot many muskrats, and few are the areas in this region where shooting *could* adequately substitute for trapping in the annual harvest of muskrats for fur.

In any consideration of these open-water harvesting methods, we should, I think, recognize the unlikeliness of any one method being wholly suitable under all conditions. Those methods and practices that are patently undesirable need not be sanctioned in responsible fur management programs, but, at the same time, reasonable advantage should be taken of such desirable features as exist in any method or practice. Reasonability, in fact, should be our guiding objective throughout, in trying to do the best we can with what we have in seeking workable combinations of efficiency and humaneness in a pursuit that is not always either efficient or humane.

In concluding this chapter, I would emphasize the desirability of setting the right traps in the right places; of making the rounds of the muskrat traps once or twice each 24 hours or more often, if necessary; of not having more traps set than can be taken care of.

*   *   *

Some advice for beginners: Never forget that muskrats come equipped with teeth. Although a principal purpose of this chapter is to aid trappers in finding and bringing back their muskrats dead, an occasional trap victim does manage to stay alive somehow whenever air remains within reach of its nostrils. These are best killed by a sharp blow on the head with a stick or hatchet handle. Blood streaming from the ears of a limp victim after striking is convincing assurance that the killing has been done well. The alternative to doing a good job of killing is to run the risk of a stunned animal regaining consciousness in the back of a hunting coat or in a boat or in some other undesirable place. Let it be reiterated as often as need be that an outraged and functional muskrat is not pleasant company at close quarters!

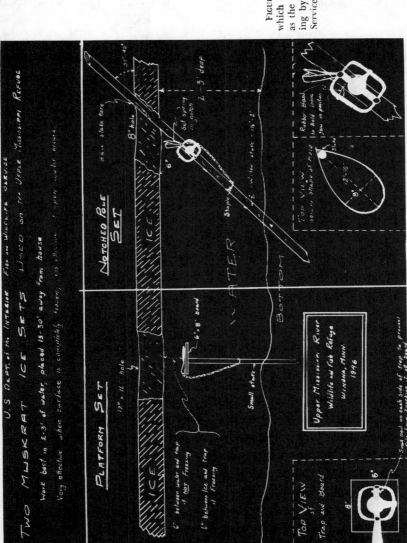

FIGURE 14. Under-ice sets in which clear ice over trap serves as the equivalent of bait. Drawing by U. S. Fish and Wildlife Service.

FIGURE 15. Indian split willow set illustrating position of trap and angle at which pole should be placed under the ice. Photos by D. E. Denmark, Hudson's Bay Company.

FIGURE 16. Left: The slanting board set can be baited. Photo by M. L. Ferguson, Iowa State College. Right: Trap used in Holland for catching muskrats in entrances of submerged burrows. Photo by Plantenzietenkundige Dienst, Wageningen, Holland.

to a little human tinkering to make them better. A few rocks rearranged or a water-logged piece of wood stuck in, and man may considerably improve on Nature for his own purposes. Nevertheless, trapping beneath the ice at burrow entrances with equipment used by most North American trappers has promise chiefly when, for some reason, the usually better sets can not be used.

Many years ago, I tried picture wire snares and choker-type wire traps at submerged burrow entrances but without success. My view at this time is that these early trials of mine were not as expertly conducted as they might have been and that non-conventional trapping devices—by which I mean devices other than common steel traps—should be worth considering for sets at burrow entrances. So many of the burrow entrances (and lodge entrances, too) that are visible through the ice from above look just about right for devices that are well designed to take swimming muskrats.

A Dutch correspondent called my attention to the trap depicted in lower Figure 16, which has been effective for trapping muskrats at burrow entrances in the Netherlands. A sample that he sent to me has powerful springs and a sensitive trigger consisting in part of a thin wire to stretch across the path of a swimming muskrat. The trap has a safety for use in setting, but no trapper should become absent-minded and feel around the set trap down in the water, as he might with a common steel trap. A mishap in this one could mean a broken hand.

Where legal to do so, muskrats may at times be stunned with club or axe while swimming under clear ice of suitable thickness. This is usually effective only in places where the shallowness of the water does not permit the muskrats to dive away from the under surface of the ice, and I have long had suspicions that injured animals escape to die.

Also, where legal, shooting through a couple of inches of ice with a .22 rifle can be satisfactory if the shooter picks his shots and does not risk merely wounding animals that swim too deeply or too fast for certain killing. The shooter should use the lowest power ammunition that is feasible (such as standard velocity shorts for killing beneath the thinner ice) and aim for the brain, both to kill cleanly and to avoid undue damage to the pelt. A high-speed long-rifle bullet could rip a large and expensive hole in a muskrat pelt. Furthermore, if the ice is so thick as to require the penetrating power of a long-rifle bullet, a person probably should not be trying to shoot muskrats through it.

Spearing of muskrats with single-pointed spears has abuses so serious that it is now illegal in many places. Among these abuses is thrusting through the sides of the smaller lodges in cold weather and wrecking the lodges in getting out the victims impaled on the spears. Spearing can also be such a convenient technique for poachers sneaking into refuges or private holdings at night that, in some localities, the mere possession of muskrat spears may fall almost in the suspicious category of possession of burglary tools. Yet, to northern trappers engaged in lodge trapping, spears may be almost indispensible in testing lodges for evidences of occupancy by muskrats, even when the spearing of muskrats may be illegal.

As in harvesting with conventional traps, much of what is good or bad about other methods depends upon the circumstances and upon what is done.

*   *   *

Burrow entrances may have their utility in trapping under the ice even when not actually used as trap sites. If their locations are known in relation to passageways of muskrats swimming from place to place, they may guide a trapper in choosing the better sites for certain types of under-ice sets. A trapper expecting to take advantage of burrow systems and passageways after the ice comes should locate and mark what he needs before rough or thick or snow-covered ice conceals too much of what lies beneath. He should not, however, count too much upon what he sees in the fall. Many burrow systems that muskrats regularly use a few weeks before freeze-up are abandoned by winter in the course of population adjustments; and a certain amount of under-ice adjustment occurs from burrow to burrow after winter definitely begins.

In my own trapping, I used an under-ice bait set that worked quite well along lake shores and stream edges (Figure 13). It never paid out for me in trapping on ordinary marshes, and I doubt that it would be effective in any food-rich habitat where the muskrats have no trouble finding all of the good food that they want. I used it most successfully under rough and clouded lake ice and in ice- and snow-covered pools of small streams—in places where ordinary methods of trapping would yield hardly any muskrats at all. It had another advantage in that it also could be used as an under-water set for minks, the discussion of which is reserved for the next chapter.

The first essential in making this set is to have a suitable site, as in the deepened channel of a burrow system for 15 to 50 feet out from the mouth of a burrow. The trap site should be where muskrats do much swimming back and forth and where the bottom is within reach of a man's arm and neither too soft for a trap bed nor too hard to push a stake into. A sandy or gravelly bottom is preferable, although a bottom of firm mud is satisfactory if the trapper takes care not to becloud the water about the set with suspended mud. "Bubble sign" under new ice may reveal just where this bait set may best be placed. After the ice has thickened, there may still be strips or small areas of ice kept thin or partly open by the passage of muskrat bodies. If the place lacks clear external "sign" indicating where the muskrats are likely to be swimming under the ice, the trapper may have to resort to whatever "muskrat sense" he has and do much chopping to try to find a prospective trap site.

My standard underwater bait was a piece of peeled potato. It was nothing of which the muskrats seemed especially fond as food. They rarely ate much of the potato bait even when they could do so without getting caught. But I generally had potatoes available at my South Dakota trapping camps, and the peeled surfaces showed up well in the darkness of the water under the ice. Although I felt that underwater visibility was more important than special flavors in attracting submerged muskrats to a set, I now would recommend trying apple, carrot, or some bait other than potato for this purpose. A carrot should be durable enough not to be easily broken, tasty enough to encourage muskrats to work for it, and conspicuous enough for them to notice under water.

A forked length of hardwood sapling is suitable for holding the bait, anchoring the trap, and marking the site. The part of the sapling below the fork should be of sufficiently small diameter to slip through the ring of the trap chain. The sapling should have a pointed end and be of the desired length to push down into the bottom to give firm anchorage. For most sets, the lower part (that is, below the fork) should be 12 to 15 inches in length. The fork should have two or three branches, so selected to cradle a piece of bait in such a way that the muskrat would have easy access to the bait from only one direction. The bait should be securely tied with string into the side of the fork that faces the direction from which a swimming muskrat is expected to approach. Then, the forked sapling, with bait in place and the lower length through the trap ring, should be pushed down until the lower part of the bait is flush with the mud or sand or gravel bottom.

The trap should be placed as close to the bait as possible and still allow the jaw action to miss striking the bait. A trapper can easily make sure that the jaws have clearance by flipping up and down the free jaw after the trap is set and in place. Ordinary long-springed No. 1 or No. 1½ steel traps are satisfactory for these sets. The spring should be turned toward the trigger side and also arranged at one side of the stake and bait, where muskrat feet would be least likely to strike it instead of the trap pan.

In my younger years, I used this set in midwinter South Dakota weather and rolled up a sleeve to do the final placing of the trap with a bare hand. Since then shoulder-length gloves have come into use for such tasks, and these gloves add to a trapper's comfort. However, I do not feel especially sorry for myself when thinking of all of my bare-handed cold-water work and the hasty wiping of tingling skin that sometimes had to be done at subzero temperatures. Once a set was made, it usually did not require more wetting of hands and arms unless it had a catch. The initial hole in the ice would be about a foot square, and the protruding parts of the sapling holding bait and trap would be left to freeze in at the side of this hole. On the next visit, a smaller hole would be cut through the new ice, so as to permit looking down through the clear water or making minor adjustments at bait and trap. Resetting the trap would require chopping the sapling free from the newer ice, lifting everything out of the water, and putting it back.

I learned early, from using this bait set, to avoid letting the body of a trapped animal rise up and freeze into the under surface of the ice in cold weather, for this could mean chopping to remove the victim or some chance of damaging the pelt. A simple way to shorten a trap chain, and thus prevent an animal from floating too high with a trap, is to push a loop of the chain through the trap spring and then run the stake through the protruding loop as well as through the ring at the end of the chain, as in upper Figure 13.

If carelessly used or used at the wrong times and places, this underwater bait set may be disappointing and more work than it is worth. At best, it seldom gave me daily catches in over 30% of the traps out. But it could still be useful under certain conditions where little else had much promise—it also might bring in two or three minks a week as a sort of bonus.

*   *   *

A considerable variety of board and platform sets may be used under the ice if conditions are right. Those of which I know function best when snow or clouded ice shuts off the light from above in the places where muskrats are swimming back and forth. The presence of a clear spot—a window of new ice—in the darker covering seems to focus the attention of muskrats, thus serving as a sort of bait, in itself. Traps should be set to catch muskrats in the act of investigating the clear spots.

One platform set has a board for the trap nailed flush on top of a sturdy stake. This (Figure 14, left) is recommended by the U. S. Fish and Wildlife Service for trapping muskrats on the upper Mississippi River at times when the surface is completely frozen. The trap should be placed six inches below the upper surface of the water when the weather is not freezing and six inches below the lower surface of the ice in cold weather.

Platforms may be draped with coontail and other submerged vegetation, and this camouflaging is probably helpful in trapping muskrats that show wariness. The smooth heads of finishing nails left sticking out of the upper surface of the platforms can prevent the traps from slipping or being too easily knocked off, yet still not hold the traps on the platforms after muskrats are caught. Baits are sometimes fastened above the trap to add to the attraction of the "windows" cut in the ice cover or in attempts to draw the muskrats to trap sites during open-water period.

Trappers of the Upper Mississippi River bottomlands have also been successful in winter-trapping by means of a notched-pole set (Figure 14, right).

Indians of the Saskatchewan Delta fasten the trap to the pole in a different manner from the above, with trap spring pointing downward and with part of the solid frame instead of the spring wedged into an axe-cut on the side of the pole (Figure 15, left). The pole with set trap is then inserted through a small hole in the ice at about the angle shown in Figure 15, right. An outstanding advantage of the notched-pole set is its effectiveness for setting in relatively deep water—up to 10 to 12 feet in depth, or even deeper, if the water frequented by the muskrats happens to be so deep. This also is a set for "windows" in the ice cover, and it can be baited.

The slanting board set is on the same principle as the above, with advantages and disadvantages of its own. I have had a fair amount of experience with it and regard it as a useful midwinter set to be placed in or near passageways of muskrats in the vicinity of big lodges or out from bank burrows. Except when suitably baited, it does not seem to work well under ice that has much light coming through from many places other than the trap holes. Its effectiveness when baited depends, naturally, upon how much the muskrats may be attracted to the baits. Nubbins of ear corn fastened to the boards above the traps were effective baits in a frozen-over pond occupied by muskrats that, before freeze-up, had habitually raided a neighboring cornfield.

Whether the slanting-board and notched-pole sets yield muskrat catches as well as they may be expected, or not, they are among the easier to use. Aside from the labor of preparing the boards or poles, of cutting holes in the ice, of walking and dragging sleds or toboggans and doing many other things that trappers do and become accustomed to doing, it may not be much of a job to put out and care for these sets. They are among the best for cold-weather trapping by people who like to keep their hands in warm, dry mittens. Boards or poles are easily chopped free from new-formed ice and pulled out of the holes for the removal of the trapped muskrats or the resetting of traps.

All of the sets so far described in this chapter show, with or without baits, so much variability in results for individual trappers that I am reluctant to predict how they would perform for anyone. Ordinarily, the trapper who knows his muskrats can make a fairly shrewd guess as to his chances under the conditions he sees before him. Sometimes there do not seem to be *any* answers to a trapping problem after the winter's ice thickens—as when the muskrats of a central Iowa ditch feed upon their stored corn for weeks without coming out of their burrows. Sometimes, even when the muskrats move in and out of their safe retreats, they may not do much of it, or they may be active only in places where they need not go near traps that are put out for them. Deep under the layers of ice, in the deepened channels and chambers, or amid the frosty air spaces and partly frozen mud and remaining puddles of water of a marsh edge or stream bank, the muskrat's world is a different world from man's and one into which man may find it hard to intrude.

*   *   *

One of the popular winter sets of expert muskrat trappers in our north-central region is made in "feed houses." It works best early in the winter, while the ice is fairly thin to cut through with axe or chisel and the outer openings of the passageways into the feed houses are readily to be found. Early winter is also most likely to be the time when feed houses are in regular use by the muskrats.

The feed houses may be no more than little roofs of vegetation over holes in the ice with "wet" water beneath. They range upward in size to the smaller dwelling lodges. Ordinarily, they are small heaps of vegetation with inner chambers or sitting places for one or two muskrats. They are often thin-walled and abandoned by the muskrats in cold weather—although muskrats may keep certain feed houses functional long after the other feed houses are abandoned and tight-frozen. By midwinter in a cold climate, most feed houses may be too little used by the muskrats (as well as surrounded by too-thick ice) to offer good trap sites.

The trapper, in distinguishing between feed houses and dwelling lodges, may be less interested in classification details than in how suitable a given structure is for a trap site—and this may depend upon legalities. If it is illegal to open the structure from the outside but legal to make any set that can be made by inserting a trap up through a natural entrance, many of the structures intermediate in size between the larger feed houses and the smaller dwelling lodges must be ruled out simply because a trapper can not reach in far enough to place a trap properly.

The likeliest feed houses for early winter trap sites are those of medium-small sizes, of sufficiently sturdy construction to withstand, if need be, the struggles of a trapped animal that may not drown. Heavy "sign" under the ice is always reassuring: the well-used watery paths marked by bubbles, floating droppings and fragments of newly-cut vegetation, now and then a live muskrat swimming past through bubbles and loose debris. If an entrance to a feed house is distinguishable, the trapper may cut a hole in the ice directly above it. Or a slushy place next to a feed house

on snow-covered ice may suggest where to try cutting
through. Or it may be necessary to cut a series of holes all
around the base of a feed house and to reach through each
hole to feel underneath. (This may not be at all uncomfortable if one wears a shoulder-length rubber glove.) After
finding a submerged entrance under a hole cut in the ice
next to a feed house, the trapper reaches up into the inner
chamber. It is a hand-and-elbow job, best done by a long-
armed man, and even a long-armed man may need to get
his shoulder close to the surface of the water to reach far
inside.

Either "stop-losses" or common steel traps may be used
for setting in the chambers of the feed houses. If using a
common steel trap, the trapper should prepare the trap
bed so that the set trap lies close to the landing and about
four inches below the surface of the water. A muskrat
would thereby be more likely to be caught by a hind leg
as it climbs out of the water. With a "stop-loss," the
trapper should simply set in the best place for catching
muskrats, without trying to catch by a hind leg. The trap
stake should be pushed down through the hole cut in the
ice over the entrance through which the trapper reaches
to set the trap.

In appraising the effectiveness of feed house sets, it
should be remembered that many feed houses are used
by single muskrats. When that is the case, the capture of
the muskrat that "owns" a feed house just about finishes
the muskrat trapping possibilities for that feed house. On
the other hand, several muskrats may be taken from a
favorite feed house used in common by several muskrats
or from one of the smaller dwelling lodges having chambers that a trapper can reach from beneath the ice. It is
usually difficult to endanger the next year's breeding stock
by setting in the trappable feed houses alone unless the
trapping efforts are unusually prolonged. There are almost

certain to be some occupants of the larger dwelling lodges that do not frequent the surrounding feed houses. The method has about the right blend of efficiency and inefficiency to permit ready harvesting of about those proportions of a muskrat crop that ordinarily should be harvested from north-central marshes in early winter.

About 90% of the muskrats taken in our experimental feed house trapping after freeze-up were found drowned when common No. 1½ steel traps were used and when the water was about 12 inches in depth in the vicinity of the feed houses. Perhaps a dozen muskrats escaped after "wring-offs" in the trapping of 285 under such conditions, and most of those were recaught soon after escaping. The common steel traps showed up far more badly in feed house trapping in shallow water covered with ice: over 40 muskrats escaped by wringing during the experimental taking of not many more than 100. Such escapes by wringing were practically eliminated by the use of "stop-losses," even though up to half of the victims did not find sufficient water in which to drown in the interiors of the shallow-water feed houses.

It is admittedly harder to make drown sets inside of the feed houses with either common steel traps or "stop-losses" than in open-water trapping on the outside. Victims caught inside have better chances of avoiding drowning by climbing up on something, on vegetation entangling the trap chains, on the surface of the ice outside, or on top of wreckage of the flimsier feed houses.

A recommended procedure to reduce losses and suffering of undrowned animals in winter trapping in feed houses is for someone to walk about on the ice during intervals between the regular trap "runs," just to kill and remove trapped animals that manage to break out of the sides of the feed houses or otherwise reach open air. In large-scale trapping by a crew of men, such activity might well keep one member profitably occupied, especially during mild thaws when ice and feed houses soften and muskrats exposed to the weather are unlikely to freeze.

A big difficulty in winter feed house trapping is due to the trapper not being able to see what he may be doing inside. Many times, after feeling around, preparing the trap bed, and setting the trap by means of a rubber glove, I have felt sufficiently dissatisfied to pull off the glove, roll up my sleeve, and finish the set bare-handed. Using bare hands, one may judge where the surface of the water is with respect to the trap and be more certain of having skimmed away floating pieces of vegetation that might clog the trap jaws.

But, aside from the discomfort of cold water and the chapping and cuts that over-much bare-handed work may invite, there *can* be feed houses into which one might not enjoy putting bare hands under any circumstances. When muskrats may be dying from hemorrhagic disease or tularemia or something unknown and I stick my hand up through mud and muddy water into chambers having dead muskrats (including some that come apart easily in fingers before I recognize what they are), I would much prefer at least the psychological comfort of having my hand encased in waterproof rubber.

A rubber glove also confers some protection against a hostile act by a live muskrat. Although a muskrat can bite through rubber if it takes aim and really clamps down, a rubber glove may deflect the more glancing of bites or provide a loose-fitting covering for a muskrat to bite into. (Let me emphasize once more that muskrat bites are not necessarily trifling; they can expose knuckle joints, cut nerves, blood vessels, and tendons, lay open the sensitive tissue under finger nails, and give the receiver troublesome wounds even when the biters, themselves, are healthy.)

As a rule, a trapper need not worry about being bitten by free and uninjured muskrats remaining in feed house or small lodge chambers unless he is trapping in a region where there might be helpless young in a nest guarded by a parent muskrat. Usually, the muskrat leaves the feed house as soon as the trapper starts working there, and I slosh below the plunge hole to advertise my coming before reaching up to continue with the trap setting. In Iowa, I know of two instances of free muskrats remaining in the chambers of feed houses to attack hands of trappers groping around them, but, in both instances, the trappers had inadvertently blocked the only escape routes of the animals.

After feed house sets are made, the trapper should be careful about putting a hand near them as long as living trapped animals may be awaiting. He should watch for tipoffs as he approaches feed house sets. If the new ice over a hole having a trap stake is clear, with perhaps a few small bubbles, the "sign" does not suggest a catch—though it may not actually prove that there is no catch. If there are bubble masses or thick air spaces under the new ice, then maybe. . . . If new ice has not formed, and the water of the stake hole is roily or has considerable floating vegetation in it, then also maybe. . . Or the water in the hole may be seen to move in a meaningful way as one approaches. Or the tip of a bamboo pole used as a stake may vibrate in the air quite independently of the wind.

Even if there is no visible outside "sign" of a catch, the trapper should at least test the trap chain before he reaches his hand up toward the out-of-sight trap. If the chain is taut or if there is perceptible movement, the trapper should do whatever is necessary—whether gently working the victim down through the plunge hole toward the outside or enlarging the passageway under the water or chopping through the side of the feed house—at any rate, to watch out for a muskrat suddenly appearing at close range and showing teeth and fight.

If the feed house trapping is done right, the great majority of the muskrats in the traps should drown shortly after being caught, and thus be unable to suffer further, to escape, or to bite trappers' hands. A trapper having indifferent success in drowning his catches may experiment a little. He may, for example, put down an extra stake to entangle a trap chain outside of the entrance of the feed house. A muskrat staying alive in a trap for any considerable time may swim around outside of the feed house as well as struggle inside, and any device preventing it from returning to the chamber makes drowning almost certain in ice-covered water.

* * *

Trapping in the chambers of the larger lodges may be either one of the best or one of the worst methods of harvesting muskrats in cold weather. Illegal over much of the United States and Canada, it is, elsewhere on our continent, not only legally permitted but also recommended by some of the most enlightened of conservation agencies. Obviously, questions of what is done, and where, need consideration.

Several main types of wintering lodges are to be found in north-central United States, and their potentialities as trap sites vary accordingly.

Ordinarily, the lodge has a large central chamber and a bed on which muskrats sit and three or four plunge holes and submerged passageways leading to the surrounding water. If built out away from shore on bottom covered by water, the usual building material is of stems of rushes and cattails, with some root material mixed in, together with miscellaneous objects such as bivalve shells, stones, and sticks, and relatively little mud. Its outer form is that of a hay cock. Occasionally, a big lodge of this type has two separate chambers—so separate, indeed, that one chamber may be in use as a mink retreat (with plunge holes frozen and the chamber accessible to minks via a hole to the outside air) at the same time that the other chamber is kept warm, protected from outer air, and in regular use by muskrats. If the lodge is double, in the sense of two separate lodges having been built so close together that they join, the chambers may be connected by either a submerged passageway or by a direct tunnel extending straight across from chamber to chamber.

To reach the chamber of the ordinary lodge for trap setting, one must cut directly through side wall or top. Care should be taken to choose a place for cutting that would be least likely to weaken the lodge. It should be, too, a place that could be plugged satisfactorily. An axe may be one of the most useful all-around tools for this cutting, though a lodge with a soft wall may be cut into with a hay knife. Some trappers prefer an ice chisel for penetrating frozen material. An opening cut fairly well down on the side of a lodge is preferable in that the vegetation will not fall from the cut into the trap. A lower hole is also better repaired by the muskrats surviving in a lodge after the trap is taken up. However, a small to medium-sized lodge having a solid, cohesive top may sometimes be opened for trap setting by cutting through all around the lower edge and then lifting up the entire top and replacing it like a lid after setting the trap.

Expert trappers may have tricks by which they give a muskrat caught in a common steel trap a good chance to drown in plunge hole or submerged passageway—such as by fastening a trap chain on a pole in the right way and slipping pole with attached chain down into a plunge hole beside a bed inside of a big dwelling lodge. Nevertheless, I do not think that common steel traps should be used

in lodge sets. When these are set in chambers within convenient human reach of holes cut in the sides of the lodges,
they may be shamefully productive of "wring-offs," even
when visited several times each 24 hours.

In my opinion, it took the "stop-loss" design of traps
to give respectability to trapping inside of large and
medium-sized lodges. Drowning rates are high with sets
that encourage muskrats encumbered by "stop-losses" to
get down into the water of the plunge holes.

The last thing to do in making a set in a wintering lodge
on a northern marsh is to plug the opening. If a solid block
(such as one originally cut out of the hole) is used as the
central plug, the edges may be sealed with wet vegetation
from the interior of the lodge or packed with snow. A good
repair may be made by fitting loose pieces in the cut hole
so that they are firm and tight, then reinforcing with an outside packing of snow. If the opening from the outside to
the lodge chamber is so big that pieces of vegetation from
the trapper's plug might be accidentally pushed into the
chamber, a little barrier of sticks may be erected to hold
back the repair material. Just two or three properly placed
sticks may be helpful.

As distinguished from the typical "hay cock" lodges
with central chambers, large lodges with flattened tops and
immense bases are sometimes seen. They often consist of
well-rotted, punky vegetation, with fresher vegetation
being used for repairs. They may have diameters of perhaps
10 feet, heights of one-and-one-half to two feet, and a half
dozen or more chambers arranged so that they connect
with each other in a ring following the outer rim of the
lodge. Such chambers may be easily reached from the outside by the trapper but do not offer especially inviting trap
sites. For one thing, these are lodges more of the shallower
parts of marshes and tend to be visited by relatively few

muskrats. Then again, it may be hard to pick strategic trap sites from the many places at which traps could be set.

Another kind of lodge is almost characteristic of the mud margins of many north-central marshes. Built of mixed vegetation and mud, stones, old bones, and whatever else the muskrats can find and carry, it is a familiar sight at the shore end of a channel leading from water-covered shallows. Often it is only a heap over a burrow that leads on under the surface of the mud to a chamber in the bank. One of these lodges may lack a chamber, or its chamber may be but an incidental sort of retreat, which swimming muskrats use or by-pass as they choose. Or the mud lodge is used mainly for the storage of duck potatoes, which are packed tightly in blind pockets, perhaps to be eaten later by hungry muskrats, perhaps not. Or, the mud lodge may be a *bona fide* lodge furnishing living quarters at the end of a channel, with bed and plunge holes like those of lodges built deeper in the marsh, or possibly with only a single plunge hole and passageway between chamber and channel.

One type of lodge, of which the outer appearance may be deceiving, is built on the ice or in the shallow water of an open slough. It may be built of weeds or submerged water plants, such as coontail or algal growths. In size, it may vary from a little push-up on the ice to a lodge several feet in height or diameter and externally resembling a real marsh lodge. Upon opening, however, a trapper may find the interior so eaten away that only an outer shell remains to cover the water hole. Sometimes, the enclosed water hole is as big as a wash tub, with sitting places for muskrats restricted to ice shelves or to a narrow border around the edge of the water hole.

Such thin-walled structures may be easily ruined if the trapper breaks the inner coatings of ice that hold the shells together. They may then more quickly collapse during thaws, or, in cold weather, extensive breaks may be more than the muskrats can repair. Where so much eating of the interiors occurs, the muskrats are probably short of food or material for repairs, anyway. Or, if the parts that are out of convenient reach of the muskrats are damaged, the animals may not be able to repair them without hazardous activity outside. Of course, if the occupants are so badly situated that winter-killing is bound to be severe, "salvage trapping" could have a certain economic justification, irrespective of destruction of the flimsier lodges.

Lodge sets should not be used in places where the trapping coincides with the time when young muskrats are being suckled unless the biggest problem in muskrat management is keeping down the numbers of muskrats—as it can be in certain areas. Such sets can be selectively deadly for females having nests containing young.

At the opposite extreme of deadliness, good results should not be expected from lodge sets if the water beneath the ice recedes away from the lodges and the muskrats live in improvised nests in air spaces or partly wet channels. The animals then may not go near the old lodge chambers until forced back by melt waters. If a trapper looks down into an opened lodge and sees the dry bed and the dry plunge holes leading into the subsurface darkness and frost crystals over everything, and there do not seem to be any promising trap sites—well, that may be about it.

Trapping in the lodges, in short, requires about as much care and headwork for good results as does any method of muskrat trapping. In my South Dakota experience as a young man, I saw many lodges ripped apart or with holes in sides or tops poorly plugged after traps were set. Even after making allowances for my early misconceptions as to how serious these disturbances could be for the muskrats, it is still true that the more irresponsible treatment of lodges is nothing to be condoned in well-conceived trapping programs. Lodge trapping may nevertheless be advantageous on large marshy holdings where some responsible agency is in a position to supervise. To my knowledge, it has worked out splendidly on the vast fur management areas of the Hudson's Bay Company and the Manitoba government in harvesting muskrats during late winter and early spring, as well as in midwinter experimental trapping carried on by the U. S. Fish and Wildlife Service in some of the north-central states.

* * *

Years ago, Dr. Ward M. Sharp, of the U. S. Fish and Wildlife Service, told me about a cold-weather set used in trapping muskrats on the Red Rock Lakes in southern Montana (Figure 18). Following is the information that he obligingly supplied for this chapter.

The set is especially adapted for those northern areas where not only do the laws forbid disturbance of the muskrat lodges but forbid also the setting of traps close to the lodges. What it does is to furnish for trap sites the equivalent of artificial lodges placed strategically on the ice over travel lanes at distances of 20 to 100 feet from muskrat-occupied natural lodges.

In general, the same locations that would be promising for slanting board and notched-pole sets should be suitable for the Red Rock Lakes ice set—almost any places where muskrats swim regularly and leisurely and exploratively under thick ice. The actual distances that sets are made away from natural lodges have less relation to effectiveness than may nearness to well-used travel routes.

The artificial lodge for the trap site is a wooden box, about 12 inches wide, 16 inches long, and 10 to 12 inches high, made out of rough lumber. A loose-fitting lid should be made for the upper opening of the box, and the lower opening should be placed over a hole cut through the ice.

This hole in the ice should be about 10 by 14 inches in size at the surface of the water. An ice ledge should be left about six to eight inches below the surface of the water to give muskrats something on which to climb and to provide a bed for the trap. The trap chain should be stapled securely to the inside of the wooden box nearest the submerged ice ledge, so that the trapped muskrat soon drowns and thus permits other muskrats to use the shelter between visits by the trapper.

The water in the hole under the box may to some extent be kept open in cold weather by activities of the muskrats within, but, if snow is available, it should be heaped over the box for insulation.

*   *   *

Nowhere in this chapter do I imply that trapping muskrats after freeze-up is easy. Trapping methods requiring much cutting by hand through thick ice or frozen mud or vegetation can hardly be other than much work. The point is that muskrat trapping can still be done after freeze-up and that, in most places, it can still be done well by people who know how and are willing and able to work at it.

CHAPTER IX

Something About Minks and Mink Trapping

THE NORTH AMERICAN mink is a member of the weasel family and a rather close relative of the land weasels and ferrets. It is a good swimmer and diver but not anywhere nearly as expert in the water as the muskrat. In fact, it is more a land animal than a water animal—a land animal that likes the water, too. Perhaps, we should call it more an animal of the water's edge. It also ranges in the woods and over meadows and pastures if it feels like it. Within limits, it goes where it wants to, but usually shows preferences for wetlands—from brooks and tile flows and creeks and drainage ditches to marsh edges and lake shores and islets.

The mink may give the impression of being a chronic wanderer, but the studies of its movements that have been carried on show that this wandering is not as nomadic as it appears. Even when the mink covers a lot of ground—I once followed for about 10 miles the trail of a mink laid down during the previous night—it tends to restrict its movements to familiar areas. Inside of these areas, it investigates this or that or travels here or there, but it still acts as if it knows where it is and what it is doing.

There are times of year when a considerable amount of traveling in strange places may be done by minks. During the mating season of late winter and early spring, minks show up far from their known retreats of the earlier parts of the winter. Midsummer to fall is a time when the season's young go forth in the world to seek their fortunes. Also, such a free agent as a mink may well be expected to change its accustomed center of activity to some extent if for any reason it happens to like one place less or another place more and nothing discourages it from making the change.

As a rule, the female minks have the smallest and most definite home ranges. Sometimes, a female of recognizable identity spends a whole winter in one corner of a marsh or in the vicinity of a certain bend of a river. Lake-shore springs that are packed full of dead or desperate fishes may be especially attractive to such minks. When these or other favored local retreats are deeply covered by snowdrifts, the minks may simply live in the drifts, coming out or not coming out on the surface. Even the males, which are the ones that track up the countryside if any do, may "hole-up" for a few days at a time in a snowdrift over a spring—or, better yet, in a muskrat lodge having dead muskrats within. Still, no one should ascribe more definite rules to mink behavior than exist. If a well-fed wild mink has energy to use up, it will use it. We see in the snow the evidences of the tireless bounding, the cruising among the muskrat lodges, the running in and out of holes, the exploration of ice heaves, root tangles, and patches of open water at times of so much food about that the active minks could not possibly have been driven by hunger.

Although minks may live in many places having few or no muskrats—for example, along high mountain streams and along the rockier of lake shores—and there are good muskrat marshes that are minkless, an almost-permissible generalization would be that the minks live where the muskrats live. At any rate, the environmental overlapping of the two species is considerable. For our north-central region, the further generalization could be made that the best muskrat marshes are at the same time the best mink marshes, even though the minks may seldom get out in the deeper tracts of the marshes until freeze-up or drought-exposure makes the deeper tracts more easily accessible.

And, although the minks appear to be as fond of muskrat flesh as of any food likely to appear in their diets, any assumptions that minks are attracted in large numbers to the best muskrat marshes primarily to prey upon muskrats are more than a little shaky. On some of our north-central marshes that are well-populated by both minks and muskrats, careful studies may bring out no evidence of the minks either killing or eating muskrats for months at a stretch, either in warm or in cold weather. Natural emergencies or population crises or epidemics among the muskrats that now and then give local minks opportunities to feed upon large quantities of muskrat flesh come just now and then, but these furnish no *regularly* available sources of food that minks have any way of anticipating.

Day by day, and month by month, minks may subsist upon food that tends to be far more abundant and available to them than muskrat flesh: crayfishes, frogs, snakes, water insects, plus whatever biological windfalls may be forthcoming in the form of land or water birds, mice, rabbits, ground-squirrels, fishes, grasshoppers, and so on. Animal life serving for varying periods of time as staple prey for minks may not always be especially abundant. It may simply be unlucky on a large scale or present in greater quantity than its environment can accommodate, whether it be fishes during a freeze-out or crippled coots starving on the ice or something else that finds itself in trouble.

Most of the mink's staple food and much of what else it feeds upon according to its occasional opportunities may be found on or about a typical north-central marsh at times when muskrats may be totally absent. But, so many times, it is to be seen that, when the muskrats go into a decline on an Iowa or Dakota or Minnesota marsh, the minks *may* (not always) decline, too; and that when the muskrats come back, so may (again, not always) the minks. These patterns may be followed even at times when muskrats are not occurring in the diets of the minks, at all.

This brings us to the idea that a good muskrat marsh may be to some extent a good mink marsh because of the engineering activities of the muskrats. As makers of prospective mink dens, the muskrats far outdo the other diggers and builders on marshes and lakes and streams and river oxbows. In winter, the passageways of the muskrats may provide the minks with their main access to waters rich in mink foods lying beneath thick ice.

The mink, as a species, *can* do without muskrat habitations to use for denning. It can use ground-squirrel burrows, badger holes, beaver lodges, cavities under tree roots, or cracks in rock faces as dens, either for individual refuges at any time of year or for the rearing of young in spring and early summer. Without being much at creative endeavor in making living quarters for itself, the mink can be quite accomplished at breaking and entering if it has something into which to break and enter. A muskrat burrow system that has been vacant for a short time is about ideal from the standpoint of the mink—especially the sort of burrow system that would be reoccupied and repaired from time to time by the muskrats. Muskrat burrows left unrepaired for more than a year or two lose attractiveness and habitability for minks. This is, if anything, still more true of unrepaired muskrat lodges used as mink dens. Compared with burrows in firm soil, lodges are much the flimsier retreats for minks or other poor housekeepers to take over.

The partiality shown by minks for denning and rearing their young in dry chambers of muskrat burrows is to be seen even about small headwaters—the brooks and pasture creeks and tile flows where muskrats occur sparsely and irregularly. Again and again, the minks select the muskrat burrows for their own den sites, until these deteriorate into uselessness for minks. Along marsh edges, the boring by the minks, the caving in of the turf, the washing in of mud from above, the digging of dogs, raccoons, etc., into old burrows, and the rehabilitating activities of the muskrats may continue in rotation over the years. Shallow-water or dry-marsh muskrat lodges may shelter an occasional litter of young minks, but such sites are seldom as safe or as popular with the minks of our north-central areas as are the bank burrows. Often such lodges are old and weed-grown, and the minks resort to them when few alternative sites are available.

During the cold weather months, muskrat habitations invite intrusions by minks not only because of their passage-ways to water beneath the ice but also because the deepened channels of the entrances and plunge holes concentrate some of the aquatic life on which minks feed. A squirming mass of air-gulping bullheads in a muskrat lodge is an understandable attraction to a mink. Sometimes, the muskrat channels lead near pockets of hibernating frogs so great that the minks carry out hundreds of the frogs and pack them in snowdrift tunnels overlying the muskrat burrows. Heaped latrines of mink droppings consisting almost entirely of remains of one kind of prey—whether of crayfish shells or the bones and scales of minnows or the indigestible parts of water beetles or dragon fly larvae or something else—signify in their own way the rather special feeding opportunities that may await minks down there in or out from the muskrat plunge holes.

It is not necessarily true that the minks *must* have all of this convenient access to aquatic food. They do not always have anything like this, and minks may winter by hunting and scavenging in the shore zones of lakes or marshes or on dry land without often getting near any water. They are adept at finding food somewhere. But, in common with many other mammals, minks seem more disposed to tolerate more crowding by their own kind when living under conditions of ease and plenty. Let it be emphasized that the number of minks that the minks themselves tolerate locally may have a decided bearing upon the number of minks living there.

*   *   *

Most minks are by nature solitary animals over most of the year. Apart from the times that mature males and females are together during the breeding season, about the only close association that wild and free-living minks *usually* tolerate are those of mother-and-young family groups in summer and—sometimes—fall. An old-timer river man once wrote me about having seen in winter a half-dozen minks traveling together like a pack. Presumably this was a family group that held together extraordinarily long.

My own observations indicate that mink litters split up and the members go their own private ways well before the coming of winter—anywhere from the middle of June to the middle of August in the north-central region. The last minks that I ever saw together late in summer looked and acted like mothers still being trailed by one or two of their grown young. Glimpses of family life among minks in the wild suggest that the splitting of the weaned litters is the culmination of increasingly frequent quarreling until, finally, the animals can no longer stand each other's company.

It is unrealistic to think of minks as being fiends or as incarnations of blood-lust or as possessors of any attributes that natural wild animals do not have. People like to exaggerate and to judge wild creatures according to human moral standards that no one should expect either the minks or their prey to adhere to. Minks are only flesh-blood-nerve-bone-and-fur wild animals, living according to their adaptations. They live for themselves with what they have to live with, as other wild animals do. They are restless and high-strung though unimaginative animals, ready killers when having opportunities for killing, responsive to situations of the moment. They can show both curiosity and indifference, boldness and wariness.

It would be reasonably accurate to regard the minks as professional fighters that are possessed of some discretion. At times, they seem intentionally to avoid places frequented by foxes and dogs. Their attitudes toward certain muskrats or groups of muskrats that are disposed to attack minks on sight can be downright practical. No one should assume that minks, professional fighters though they are, care nothing about wounds nor that minks experienced in the ways of formidable muskrats feel impelled to risk severe bites just for the sake of a meal if they can feed upon something else more cheaply. Although the minks may not figure out things in detail, the old ones at least seldom behave like dumbheads. If a mink overtakes a panicky muskrat trying to run away on the ice, killing may be easy. If a big muskrat goes after a mink with mayhem in mind and carving tools in front, the mink may not care to accept the sporting challenge.

After all, minks eat every day, or try to, and, while they are tough and can take punishment, their predatory activities are geared to a year-after-year basis. I have examined the bodies of a number of free-living minks that were obviously several years old, and I doubt if they would have lasted as well as they did if they had permitted themselves to be laid open with any regularity by the weapons of their victims.

It is in the old story of mink versus mink that we see minkish nature most clearly reflected. Day-by-day patterns of living alone and leaving alone may be interrupted by fights. Sometimes, the area fought over by well-matched minks may be extensive—two that I measured had total areas of around 500 square yards of snow mussed up like sites of boys' hockey games. In another place, where a big mink overtook another of equal size, the two fought it out in a space of two square yards, leaving the tufts of mink fur and blood drops thoroughly kneaded into the packed snow beneath. Plenty of down-to-business giving and taking went into that one, but each mink left under its own power.

Despite minkish durability, a mink may be found dead of its fight wounds now and then during any time of the year. We can thus account for some of the natural self-limiting that occurs in mink populations. On areas with which I am most familiar in Iowa and eastern South Dakota, the highest mink populations seem to level off naturally, by early winter, at 12 to 20 per square mile in superior marshes. Poorer environments have correspondingly lower numbers of minks. In good or poor mink country, there seem to be fairly definite population thresholds. Below these thresholds, minks tend to keep out of serious trouble with other minks; above them, more frequent encounters may provoke fighting.

Nevertheless, it can be repeatedly seen from the snow "sign" that not all minks fight whenever they have a chance to fight. Many minks prudently yield right-of-way to other minks, keep out of holes occupied by other minks, and withdraw to their own privacies as if they knew what was good for them. On a square mile of marsh having a dozen minks, the individuals are surely aware of the proximity of other minks on far more occasions than are manifested by fights or by any overt acts, but their lack of toleration may still keep them pretty well spread apart and thus have its influence on the population levels that an area may accommodate.

The deadliness in relations of this sort may lie not so much in minks killing minks in direct attack as in gradually, perhaps bloodlessly, forcing withdrawals of the "surplus" minks into less favorable places. There, something drastic and final—as through the agencies of large birds of prey, foxes, dogs, automobiles, etc.—is more apt to befall them. An individual mink's world may have much in it that is biologically "off limits."

Two of the minkiest places that I studied closely in Iowa were Round Lake in 1935 and Wall Lake in 1953. Round Lake had five females with young localized along about a mile of shore line during that particular summer, or a total of probably more than 30 individuals as of late summer, yet certainly no more than half as many remained on the 450-acre marsh by freeze-up. The most mink-crowded part of Wall Lake in the summer of 1953 was a tract of about 40 acres of meadow with shallow-water indentations. This tract had at least six female minks with their litters of young, or probably an average of about a mink per acre at weaning time. By late fall, it is doubtful if more than 20 minks were left on the whole marsh of nearly 1,000 acres, despite highly attractive conditions for the species.

We thus see that Nature does not stock-pile minks either.

* * *

The old-time trappers and naturalists made no mistake when they noted that the mink can be closely associated with the muskrat and that muskrat flesh can be, on occasion, a prominent item of the mink's diet. These conclusions hold up well in our day. What do not hold up well when examined from the viewpoint of our present information are some old assumptions about just what mink relations with muskrats mean in terms of more muskrats or fewer muskrats.

Among the more sweeping assertions on this subject are those that a mink can go in and clean out a whole colony of muskrats when it wants to. That the losses to trappers and the fur industry resulting from a mink killing muskrats far outweigh the fur value of the mink itself. That a mink is a bloodthirsty villain deserving to be wiped off the face of the earth or, at the least, confined to a pen on a fur farm. A lot of this reflects only the immoderation that man too often shows toward wild creatures arousing his displeasure. It reflects also the difficulty with which certain facts are correctly recognized and understood.

As was brought out earlier in the book, scavenging by minks upon dead muskrats may be responsible for some of the misconceptions concerning mink predation held by trappers, game wardens, and naturalists, especially when muskrats die of disease during the colder months. Minks may be adept at finding dead muskrats at such times, whether the die-offs are wide-spread or localized. Among the outside manifestations of a die-off are groups of musk-rat lodges or burrow systems with unrepaired mink holes, trails showing where minks dragged dead muskrats over the snow, blood and bones and fur and about everything else that might *look* like predation. If someone cut open the lodges during a die-off, he might find dead muskrats in the chambers, partly eaten or not eaten at all by minks. The muskrats may lie as they died—in almost any position from lying on backs with feet in the air to huddling in groups having the appearance of peaceful sleeping—or as the minks left them after pulling them around or stacking them in the lodge chambers.

It should not do any harm to re-emphasize that the killing of muskrats by minks that does occur may not be anywhere nearly as much in competition with muskrat trapping as trappers commonly believe. When a trapper knows enough about both minks and muskrats to recognize

Figure 17. Of man and musk-rats in the Canadian North. Photos by D. E. Denmark, Hudson's Bay Company.

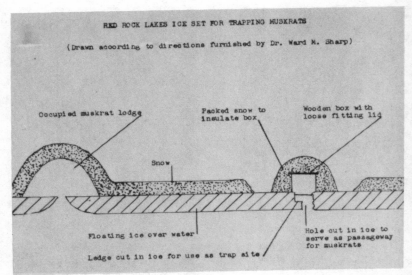

FIGURE 18. Wooden box set for use on ice near muskrat habitations. Courtesy U. S. Fish and Wildlife Service.

FIGURE 19. Mink drowned in "stop-loss" trap. Photo by M. L. Ferguson, Iowa State College.

"population symptoms" and the special kinds of handicaps under which muskrats live at times that they are preyed upon by minks, he also is in a better position to distinguish between the mink predation that counts and the mink predation that does not count from the standpoint of his own fur returns.

In one way, mink predation upon muskrats may be summed up with the generalization that the majority of muskrats falling victim to minks would not hold any notable promise of profit for trappers if the minks did not get them. The social misfits and excess male muskrats that minks prey upon from late winter to spring—and which otherwise might be harvested by trappers—often are of low commercial value because of the large number of wounds that their pelts receive from other muskrats. Of still lower commercial value are the newly weaned young muskrats of sorts that are most vulnerable to minks during the summer months—the trapper has no use for them at all unless they grow up.

"But," I can hear someone say, "if they grew up, those young muskrats *would* have commercial value when the trapping season came around. If the minks were killed off, they couldn't kill the young muskrats, and, if the minks didn't kill them, the young muskrats *would* grow up!" The big flaw in this reasoning is its neglect of the fact that the young muskrats that minks can prey upon tend to be animals of such poor life-expetancies, *anyway,* as to stand little chance of being alive by the trapping season, whether minks get them or they die from other causes. The distinction should be made that a great deal of the mink predation upon them takes place only *incidentally* to Nature's own annual shaking down of muskrat populations to fit the environment available to muskrats.

A lot of biological wastage in muskrat populations could be prevented by maintaining the environment of the muskrats in suitable condition for them and by keeping the muskrat populations within the limits that are suitably accommodated by their environment. If these things are done, the mink predation usually diminishes to negligible proportions, even when plenty of minks are around and willing to eat muskrats at every opportunity.

Furthermore, the fur laws permitting, a trapper may often effectively compete with minks for the surplus muskrats by doing his muskrat trapping *before* those muskrats become vulnerable to the minks. With the proper kind and intensity of trapping, especially in the first half of the winter, the propective mink victims of the months to come may either be converted into salable pelts or left in such comfortable circumstances by reduction of the general muskrat population so that they no longer are prospective mink victims.

In my opinion, modern fur management should strive to manage both muskrats and minks on a sustained-yield basis. The view that we may have either an abundance of muskrats or an abundance of minks—that we may not have both but must choose between one or the other—has been shown to be fallacious over and over again on our north-central study areas. As a fallacy, this one can be expensive to perpetuate when resulting, if nothing else, in the needless sacrifice of a wild fur animal as important as the mink on many marshes devoted to fur production. Reasonable trapping pressure to utilize the mink as a renewable resource is different from campaigning to get rid of it all together.

One type of genuine loss to the trapper results from minks feeding upon muskrats caught in traps. It can be rather heavy when the trapping is done carelessly or under unfavorable conditions, as on drought-exposed marshes and streams where trap victims are easily found by opportunistic minks. My own losses from this cause of years ago and those incurred in our Iowa trapping experiments averaged less than 1% of the muskrats caught in traps, even when the trapping was done in the midst of substantial mink populations. I do not see why such losses should not usually be kept down to a low figure in north-central muskrat trapping, if only through the use of good methods of trapping.

*   *   *

Possibly most Iowa trappers catch most of their minks by accident—at least during periods of open-water trapping. True, many trappers set traps in places where they have some hope or expectation of catching minks, and some of the expert mink trappers put out traps exactly where the minks stand about the best chances of getting into them. Still, it is to be suspected that, in the north-central region, most minks are caught in traps set for muskrats.

Let us now see what may be suggested to reduce the role of plain luck in open-water mink trapping.

First, from the trapper's point of view, what kind of animal is the mink to catch and to hold in a trap?

Minks can be either trap-wise or rather unwary with respect to traps. The less wary are generally young ones, and the trap-wise are generally old ones that got to be old partly because they learned about traps early. It is often contended that the coming of cold-weather winter, in itself, increases the wariness of minks toward traps. Perhaps some of the apparent differences in wariness attributed to minks is merely due to the greater ease with which mink traps are set before freeze-up. A trapper may then visit or set traps at the water's edge by means of a boat, or by wading, without leaving much human "sign" around the traps.

A trap set in the water may be sufficiently concealed to be unnoticed by most minks, particularly if rusty or stained. A good trapper is also careful to make sure that a submerged trap otherwise blends more or less into its background. A bed may be excavated so that the trap lies flat and inconspicuous on the bottom. Water-logged leaves may be draped over spring, chain, and pan, and a few over the jaws may be desirable, as well, provided that nothing interferes with the proper functioning of the trap.

The few minks caught in "stop-loss" traps incidental to our experimental trapping of muskrats in Iowa were drowned, and I see no reason why these designs of traps should not be used with confidence in drown sets for minks (Figure 19). Also, ordinary steel traps may be set for drowning trapped minks, especially if trap chains run along one-direction guide wires to deep water. Although a mink is powerful for its size, and a big trapped one that finds secure footing or something to brace against during its struggles can be more than a little hard to hold, it is not a hard animal to drown.

In the selection of trap sites for trapping minks before freeze-up, special attention should be paid to places showing *repeated* use by minks. A trapper should look for certain "key" landings along a stream bank, partly submerged and partly caved entrances to muskrat burrows, narrow passageways of many kinds, brooks and tile flows that minks like to explore. Shallow-water lodges and burrows that have been recently abandoned by the muskrats offer some of the most promising sites for mink traps. Trap sites should also be chosen so that dogs, rabbits, livestock, etc., are unlikely to get into or spoil the sets.

Some veteran professionals do well by creating their own special trap sites for minks. The important thing is to keep in mind what a passing mink is likely to do and then, within the limits imposed by mink psychology, to try to insure that the mink comes to a certain place readily and naturally.

A little tunnel with an entrance at the water's edge may be made by nailing together four narrow boards, and this may have its attractiveness enhanced by baiting. Wooden constructions should be put out long before the trapping season opens if it would be legal and feasible to do so. They may be left out on a year-around basis, so that they weather, become overgrown with vegetation, or otherwise lose their strangeness for minks. They may be especially suitable for use on land where the trapper has exclusive trapping rights. By a little baiting now and then, well-placed artificial burrows may become well-used retreats of local minks and, accordingly, desirable trap sites during the open season for mink trapping.

Mink trapping in cold weather may be done by using either drown-sets or dry-sets. Naturally, from the standpoint of humane methods, the drown-sets are preferable, and I would advocate using them wherever their use is practical.

Some of the drown-sets that take minks are the identical sets used for trapping muskrats after as well as before freeze-up. Without setting specifically for minks, one may take an occasional mink in a feed house or lodge, at a burrow entrance, or in miscellaneous under-ice sets made for muskrats. I have noticed that one of the best places to take a mink by accident is in the chamber of a feed house shortly after the feed house has ceased to be visited by muskrats.

In sets intended for minks, the under-water bait set described for muskrats in Chapter VIII—using a peeled potato—worked well for me in my midwinter South Dakota trapping. (Figure 13 has a peeled carrot instead of a potato for bait.) Minks, not being vegetarians, must be attracted to this bait by its appearance. This set was for me a regular stand-by for trapping minks along moderate-sized streams and along lake shores. It had an advantage in being a drown set and one not absolutely requiring daily visits. It would remain functional from day to day despite ordinary changes in winter weather. It would be neither conspicuous nor easily tampered with nor robbed by human meddlers, if it were made with the possibilities of meddling in mind.

On the few occasions when I had to be careful about possible fur thieves, I left a marker on shore (or some other place away from the trap site) and cut off the top of the bait holder and trap stake below the surface of the water. At each visit, I would locate the hole cut in the ice, open it up so that I could look down at the set or reach in with an arm to feel around. Before leaving, I would kick some snow in and about the hole cut in the ice and let the wind and the cold obscure the evidences of what I had done. Finally, I would fix again in mind the meaning and position of the marker away from the set.

When used for minks, alone, this set often entailed much work and many consistently empty traps. But, over the winters of my own trapping, I caught many minks with it, including a number of smart ones that had been evading my dry sets. I would rate it among the best for use under the ice.

Apart from the actual making of the set, the most important thing in using the potato-bait set for minks is selecting the site for setting. The selection does have to be right, for a set placed where a mink does not go obviously will not catch the mink.

The radius of activity of a mink working in the water under the ice away from a plunge hole may not be great. "Key" trap sites are short distances—from a foot or so to several yards—out from plunge holes that are regularly used by minks. Frequently, this means next to or out from old mink-used muskrat burrows or under snowdrifts having many mink tunnels of different ages. Snowdrift tunnels that are regularly mink-tracked with muddy or bloody water or strewn with remains of aquatic prey are most promising.

In trapping under stream-edge snowdrifts, or where the ice over springs may be thin, the mink trapper should be careful about breaking through. He should also avoid undue messing up of favorite snowdrifts of the minks, particularly in the vicinities of plunge holes. Otherwise, he may find that the drifts do not remain favorites.

In the absence of snowdrifts, minks may show partiality for holes or series of holes in the ice at the edge of streams or for mink-sized holes between ice and bank. Sometimes, an unbaited trap may be set and suitably and inconspicuously staked directly in one of these small holes, but it is a better practice, where possible, to chop a hole for the stake in the ice within trap-chain length of the mink hole. The trap should be inserted through the stake hole and under the ice so that it lies directly under the undisturbed mink hole. The best of these sets are effective at places where minks are in the habit of discarding fish heads, egg masses of frogs, and mollusk shells.

Some cautioning as to the use of these under-ice sets should be given. The trapper should always make sets that he can get out of if, by chance, he finds himself caught while feeling blindly beneath. As a youth, I once stuck a forearm into a small, smooth mink hole leading downward through about a foot of ice and got a thumb caught in the very strong No. 1 trap awaiting on the bottom. This trap had been placed by putting it directly through the mink hole, so I reasoned that, if I could get it back out that way, I would be all right. But the hole was too small to permit extraction of the trap with my thumb in it the way it was, and I was lying on the ice in an unhandy position to do extensive chopping with the hatchet. In my desperation, I somehow managed to squeeze the frame of that old-time trap (which had a heavier and sturdier frame than the ordinary No. 1 of today) enough out of shape so that I could work trap and hand up through the hole.

That was far from the last steel trap in which I ever got caught, but it was the last trap accident that was dangerous for me. Thereafter, I always had the answers in mind before feeling around without knowing whether traps were sprung or set.

*　*　*

Unfortunately, dry sets with steel traps cannot be classed among the more humane sets for minks. When the minks are so wary that it is often a real accomplishment to take one even in a concealed steel trap, I do not see how the use of any "humane" trap of bulky construction could have much promise as a substitute. The most satisfactory procedure that I worked out in my own trapping years was to use both dry sets and potato-bait drown sets in combination—each at its most suitable places—but to rely more upon dry sets during the colder parts of the winter and to use them more for trap sites that were fairly close to headquarters. In that way, if night-time cold did not bring relief to a victim, the latter at least could be dispatched on the following morning's "run."

The larger the mink, the more powerful it generally is. A three-pound male, dry-caught, can pull right out of a No. 1 or 1½ steel trap having a weak spring. Even in a trap with a strong spring, a mink's muscular foreleg may slip through the jaws until held only by the toes. If long held alive only by the palm of a foot, a mink may bite away the part of the foot below the trap jaws, then pull out and escape, most likely to die after escaping. If caught by a single toe, a mink may be expected soon to twist out, but such injuries seem to be little handicap to an escaped animal. A firm hold by *two* toes may be relatively secure, as the animal seldom either bites on so little of its foot extending beneath the trap jaws or succeeds in pulling through or twisting out the rest of the way. For dry sets for minks, I came to use almost exclusively a design of No. 1 trap having webbed jaws, with flanges preventing victims from biting close to the holding surfaces of the jaws.

If dry-trapping is justifiable at all, the trapper should do what he can to insure that traps and victims remain where they should be. In my trapping, I usually put a large spike through an opening in a chain link and drove the spike out of sight in frozen ground if the chain of a dry-set trap could not be satisfactorily stapled to a heavy root or the trunk of a tree. I never trusted a movable drag as anything on which to fasten a mink trap.

My own mink trapping, whether with drown or dry sets, was mainly based upon strategic effort. In evenings, I would lie in camp and reconstruct in my mind the "sign" of the day and consider it in relation to what I had seen earlier. Of the places that would be frequently visited by minks, I would rule out many mink-used holes in hill sides, river banks, etc., because of their use by animals other than minks. In my earlier years as a trapper, I made careful sets at such holes only to find rabbits in the traps next day. Mink holes at the surface of snowdrifts also proved to be poor trap sites, as the minks either did not return or, too often, went in and out of new holes when they did resort to the drifts. Nor, in my own trapping did I ever have much luck setting traps at the entrances of mink holes in muskrat lodges—though I learned since that I did not use these as trap sites anywhere nearly up to their potentialities. Furthermore, large numbers of these outer holes by which minks enter ground, snow, water, food-caches, or favorite retreats of any sort may be unpromising as trap sites because of what happens when snow falls, drifts, melts, or turns into ice.

These considerations reduced my top-notch dry sets for

minks to those in: (1) upper parts of muskrat burrows with small, frequently used mink holes in them and (2) the places where snowdrift tunnels converged at the entrances of holes leading underground or under the ice to water. The sites had to be in places where minks were just about compelled to go if they were to make use of favorite retreats. They had to be in places where no animals other than minks would be likely to get into the traps. They had to be in places where traps would be fairly certain to remain functional despite ordinary snow storms and weather changes. They had to be suitable for placing and concealing the traps and in which the status of the traps could be ascertained by the trapper at later visits without disrupting the sets.

In dry-setting for minks in the upper part of a muskrat burrow, I would usually cut into a well-traveled part of the burrow at a place a yard or more from the principal mink entrance, between the entrance and the water. After setting the trap so' that it would lie flush and lightly covered with shredded grass or willow leaves on the floor of the passageway, I would cover the trap-hole with some natural material, such as a flat rock or the firm shell of a weathered and partly-rotten log.

Where existing laws make cutting into burrows illegal, burrow systems that are partly caved in from natural causes may sometimes offer workable equivalents. In these, traps perhaps may be set in natural openings and the trap-holes covered in the same manner described for the artificially cut holes.

The purpose of this covering of the trap-holes is to shut out the light yet to permit lifting up the covering to peek in when need be. Also, if possible, I would leave a little kink of loose trap chain where it could easily be seen and where it positively could not remain kinked if a mink were in the trap.

The set at the converging tunnels of a snowdrift is particularly adapted for use during blizzardy weather—if the trapper has earlier marked with long poles (or by markers otherwise high in the air) the sites of the best-used holes leading under the ice or to fish-filled springs, etc. Then, when more snow is being heaped on the drifts, or blown away again, and the minks continue boring into and out of the drifts, the trapper may dig right down to the base of the drift at the spot indicated by the external marking and have some expectation of finding what he looks for.

If he finds one of these "arterial highways" of the minks, he should avoid breaking a big hole in the drift to reach it. The hole that he digs should be just big enough so that he may conveniently reach in to set the trap. Trap jaws should not be left in contact with the snow so that they freeze down. I found it advantageous to cover jaws, pan, and part of the trap spring with a couple of sections of toilet paper, the outer edges of which were weighted down with snow to freeze in position so that the paper concealed the trap without interfering with the action. After setting the trap, I would fit a solid piece of snow or ice into the break in the tunnel wall, leave a kink in the trap chain where I could later count on seeing it if I did not want to open up the tunnel again, and heap some more snow against the outside of the solid piece. I could go away, leaving the wind to blow and the outside snow to drift wherever it would. With this kind of set, it makes little difference where the mink enters the snowdrift, whether it reaches the "arterial highway" via an old hole or by digging a new one.

This all may seem like work, and it can be work. It should be remembered that the methods are those by which minks may be caught at times of year when many trappers do not think that mink trapping is worth trying. I would not think that mink trapping under conditions of constantly blowing snow would be worth trying either, if it meant putting traps out just anywhere.

For trapping man-suspicious animals having such a splendidly developed sense of smeli as the minks, I boiled the traps in lye-water from wood ashes, rinsed, dried, and then dipped them in hot paraffin to seal in the odor of the metal itself. Thereafter, I would not handle them with bare hands nor keep them in places where they would be apt to acquire undesirable odors. My footgear had rubber soles. While chopping out a trap bed or arranging vegetation at the trap site, I would kneel on my outer coat, laid with outer surface down. I knew that some human scent might linger at the trap site but reasoned that, if no concentration of scent were left on specific objects, the amount of my scent still having warning power for a mink's nose should be well diluted by the time that a mink came around.

I know, too, that trappers who have caught more minks than I have may not bother about being especially careful in their trap setting. Nevertheless, not all minks are equally wary with respect to man and man's traps, and I am merely indicating here the precautions that I learned to take in order to catch the warier ones. In the actual setting of mink traps on land, I may have been more careful than was necessary, but I did get some old-timer minks that other trappers were not getting, and I liked to feel that I was doing things well.

* * *

Mink trappers disagree among themselves as to the advantages of using baits for dry sets. I can easily see why there should be disagreement, for the experiences of even the same trappers in baiting minks may differ from year to year. In my own mink trapping, I baited sets with fish, muskrat carcasses, and other items that should have been tasty for minks but caught so few in these sets that I con- cluded that artificial baiting (except in using the under- water potato bait) did not pay. Indeed, I felt that wary minks were far more often warned than attracted by the food baits that I put out for them. So many times, the minks went on past my bait sets or approached them and turned away. Yet, in connection with experiments in Iowa, I did some baiting that minks responded to. Without set- ting or intending to set traps (but keeping in mind what I would want if I were trapping), I systematically baited certain holes under tree roots or in marsh-edge banks or in muskrat lodges with either skinned muskrat carcasses or complete bodies of muskrat victims of disease or winter- killing. Some (not all) of these artificial food caches be- came so habitually visited by minks that effective trap sites could have been made of them without difficulty. In other cases, where the minks were originally showing interest in certain retreats independently of my baiting, they also responded to new food material stuffed into the holes from time to time.

A main conclusion that I long ago came to with respect to baiting minks is that the best bet is often to let them, in effect, bait themselves. Let them pile their own fishes and frogs about the landings of plunge holes, drag in and cache their own duck and muskrat carcasses. Then, when the minks demonstrate enough partiality toward their own caches, the trapper can make his sets.

With hind-sight to help me, I now believe that I was unsuccessful in trapping minks at mink holes in muskrat lodges for three reasons: First, I wasted too many traps at holes in lodges having insufficient attraction to cause the minks ever to make return visits. Most mink-bored lodges, having but a foodless chamber and a frozen plunge hole within, are nothing special in a mink's world. Second, many of the lodges showing much mink-use, with muskrat or waterfowl remains within and latrines outside, were used as trap sites after their food caches were too thoroughly consumed by the minks to attract them to come back. Third, I am now sure that, by not placing the traps right, I spoiled some good prospective trap sites at mink holes in lodges that were still being visited by minks when the sets were made.

In trapping wary minks with dry sets, the traps may preferably be set some distance away from places subject to *particularly* close inspection by prospective victims. The place where a mink appears most apt to stop and sniff is immediately in front of a bait or food cache or in front of a hole that it is about to enter. Accordingly, if the traps can be set elsewhere, they stand better chances of being unnoticed.

From the results of our Iowa baiting experiments, a number of suggestions may be offered for improving the effectiveness of sets at mink holes in muskrat lodges. Assuming that everything about this procedure would be legal, I would suggest that a trapper look especially for mink-bored lodges having long, straight, horizontal passageways leading to the inner chambers. A passageway should not only permit one to push bait with a stick deep into the lodge but also to cut unobtrusively through the outer part of the lodge to prepare a trap site (without the trap) a foot or so inside of the outer entrance of the passageway. It need not be such a difficult job to scoop a hole out of the side of an ordinary muskrat lodge to reach the main mink passageway and to fill in the man-made hole afterward so that it differs little in appearance from the undisturbed outer covering of the lodge. After a mink-bored lodge is systematically baited until it shows evidence of regular visiting by minks, a trap may be put in.

Various scents for attracting minks to trap sites are commercially available. When I was a trapper, I invested in samples of a few of the products that were advertised in persuasively laudatory terms, but I never could credit any of these bottled scents with catching a mink for me. I am not claiming that not any of these work, for I can conceive of some that could have attractions for minks, including those based upon body secretions of the animals. The effectiveness of the latter, however, would probably be greatest during the late winter and early spring breeding season, when trappers conscientiously mindful of breeding stock probably should be through with their mink trapping, anyway.

*   *   *

Frankly, I do not wish to encourage people to become "big" mink trappers in the sense of stringing out traps over routes of hundreds of miles in settled communities and making the rounds once a week or so by car. Whether this sort of thing involves "muscling in" on other trappers or not, I do not think that it is a desirable way of trapping. Certainly, such extremely long trap lines have their wastefulness and cruelties and, certainly, they do not promote good feelings among local people who are interested in knowing who is trapping, and where, and how they themselves may be affected thereby. In my own trapping years, I never knew anyone who maintained extensive motorized traplines, but we did have hunters who worked through the countryside with dogs trained to scent minks; and local trappers were resentful indeed upon finding the dug-out mink dens and the skinned mink carcasses that these transients left behind.

Even when no private property rights are violated, when everything is completely legal, and when the trappers conduct themselves like gentlemen, tremendous catches of a public fur resource that is necessarily limited in supply may arouse resentment—and not merely because of personal jealousies. For there are questions of what is proper and equitable in fact, as well as in the law books.

What I should like to see in north-central mink trapping would be more of a combination of an amateur's philosophy and a professional's skill. In short, this book is written for people to whom following a trapline means, first of all, a wholesome and enjoyable outdoor pursuit plus some opportunity for monetary profit rather than, first of all, a business venture. The few thousands of dollars that I made as a small-time professional trapper of years ago went years ago, and, if any traces remain, I would not know where to look for them; but I do have memories of outdoor beauty and peace of mind, of freedom of living, of health, and of many intangible values that are difficult to express in any words, which I doubt that I would have now if it had not been for the trapping. Without the trapping income, I do not see how I as an individual could have afforded the economic luxury of enjoying anywhere nearly so much of the winter out-of-doors.

The minks were then much more to me than profitable prey. They were much more to me than the prizes of success in what might be called a game of wits against animals of untrusting and independent natures, carried on also against quite an array of technical problems. The minks were a part of my outdoor scene, and I want them to remain a part of the outdoor scene for other people, to be harvested as decently as possible and on a sustained-yield basis, as any other game or fur resource should be.

Although the mink, with its single annual litter per breeding female, does not have the reproductive resilience of the muskrat, the mink may maintain itself at moderate to high population levels year after year despite rather intensive human exploitation. It is not clear exactly how much reduction during the fur season a thriving mink population can withstand—possibly as high as 75% at

FIGURE 20. "Also, ordinary steel traps may be set for drowning trapped minks . . ." Photo courtesy Jim Sherman, Iowa State Conservation Commission.

FIGURE 21. "Many people . . . think back upon their youthful experiences as trappers as among the most pleasant of their lives." Photo by Iowa State Conservation Commission.

times—but it is clear that human exploitation *can* grade into overexploitation when carried on to the point of gleaning. The last minks *can* be trapped out of a locality if the trappers are expert and really go about doing it. The worst cases of overexploitation of which I know, however, are some in which the minks were systematically located with dogs and then dug out.

For practical conservation of mink breeding stock, the conscientious trapper may be advised simply to avoid taking females during the latter weeks of the mink trapping. The home ranges of the females, it may be recalled, are sometimes all but restricted to the vicinity of a spring or tile flow full of dead or air-gulping fishes or to a series of land holes or to a big stream-edge snowdrift. By the time that snow is on the ground and the local minks have been thinned down somewhat, a trapper should have a fair idea of where the small-sized (hence probably female) minks are living, often in some isolation.

CHAPTER X

About Youngsters and Outdoor Manners

As before indicated, although fur-trapping has its economic aspects, its intangible values may outweigh—sometimes far outweigh—monetary profits.

This may be especially true for youngsters. Many people in mature life think back upon their youthful experiences as trappers as among the most pleasant of their lives. Older people may discover that they have common interests with strangers or acquaintances in that they both trapped when they were young. They remember early morning breakfasts and then heading off toward the creek while still dark, to make their rounds before school. . . . Weather turning from frosty to nippy cold. . . . Open water, clear ice, snowdrifts. . . . Tracks, expectations, empty traps, and more tracks and expectations . . . then, maybe something . . . . I remember the prestige among my Junior High and neighborhood friends that my first mink brought me at the age of fourteen!

There may also be unpleasantness for young trappers, and some of the worst of trapping abuses may be those of young trappers. I have no intention of encouraging youngsters to trap if that means traps left unvisited for days at a time or set in places where all manner of luckless wildlife may get into them. One purpose of this book is to help young trappers avoid mistakes.

*   *   *

Let us consider a little more the matter of animals in steel traps. I do not think that it is wholesome for a youngster (or anyone else) to cultivate an attitude of callousness toward animals remaining alive and suffering. It is still less wholesome to justify prolonging the suffering of trap victims on the grounds of their being only stinking skunks, blood-thirsty minks, or labeled in other ways that man considers uncomplimentary. The barbarities of man in punishing wild creatures for merely being their natural selves can be senseless, indeed, and nothing to be proud about.

To be sure, the mink is a predator, an animal that may kill for a living and sometimes kill more than it needs to eat. It is an animal equipped with teeth that are adapted for little except fighting and flesh-feeding, with a digestive system adapted for the digestion of little except flesh, with a nervous system permitting only a rather narrow range of behavior. It has energy to expend and needs food to supply more energy. It responds to opportunities and to emergencies, alike, in the same fundamental ways that other wild animals do, living for itself, as it can, in the ways that it is adapted to live. Whether it kills what man wants or what man does not want, a mink is just a wild animal being itself.

Wild animals should not be thought of as either man's intentional enemies or helpers. What they do in these respects is neither morally good nor morally bad. Human morality, after all, is man's and he should concern himself with trying to live up to his own moral standards instead of imposing them upon wild creatures. As a living creature, himself, man has some justification for exploiting other forms of life, or in protecting his own intersts, but such does not justify brutality on his part.

Trapping should be made as decent as a trapper can make it and kept that way.

* * *

There are also standards of conduct that should apply to a young trapper's relations with other trappers and other people. Sometimes, in some localities, there may be dirty work—stealing of traps or furs. Everyone has personal rights but they do not include robbing someone else because of suspicions that someone else may be robbing. Neither do one's rights include illegal trapping because someone else may be doing it. A young trapper should first try to get clear facts on what actually is happening and then talk it over with adults whose judgment can be trusted.

Some of these situations may be bad enough to call for teamwork in a community. I know of an example in northern Iowa: Trappers organized to protect themselves against trap and fur thievery and they virtually eliminated the practice for a number of years. Then, the organization fell apart, and the old troubles came back, about as before. It is still human nature with which every one has to deal, but community ethics can set the pattern, and, as a member of a community, a young trapper can do his part, too.

Competition as a source of friction among trappers may be another one of the realities of life that young trappers run up against. Except on private lands, leased public lands, registered traplines, etc., licensed trappers may have equal rights in law, but it does not follow that all will be satisfied with equal opportunities. Where there is something worth competing for, there may be setting of traps at trap sites already in use by someone else, rude or threatening talk, and even totally illegal violence. When this is the sort of situation that exists, the question to be considered is whether the trapping is worth participating in by anyone who traps mostly for enjoyment of the out-of-doors.

I do not pretend to know any rules for always doing the right thing. These person-to-person relationships are not those for which answers may be neatly filed away in anyone's head in advance. It should be proper to advise youngsters to keep out of unnecessary fights—that is, real fist fights—in trapline arguments as well as in other arguments; but I do not wish to leave the impression that a youngster, through trapping, necessarily risks getting into more fights than he does in many other ordinary activities. If he looks for trouble, he can find it in too many places to enumerate here. If he conducts himself with calmness and reasonability, if he stands by his rights without lippiness, he should not have much trouble with other trappers in a respectable neighborhood. The Golden Rule is the best test of rightness and wrongness in most situations that can lead to fist fights.

* * *

Youngsters intending to trap on privately-owned or rented lands away from their home places should first obtain permission from the persons in charge. The legal aspects of trespassing differ with the area, but, even though a person is not required by law to ask a land holder for permission to trap (or to hunt or fish or pick walnuts and so on), he should ask anyway, if only for the sake of courtesy and good feeling. If a land holder is uncivil because someone asks permission in a pleasant manner, the person asking should just leave the premises without arguing. It may be perfectly true that some people have exaggerated ideas of property rights, but the land holder is still boss so far as his land is concerned. Moreover, I would advise against even thinking about sneaking in to trap (or hunt, fish, etc.) on land on which it is known that the land holder does not want anyone to do so. Whatever is done on the land of anyone else should be done above-board and with self-respect.

Once anyone is given privileges on another person's land, he should not forget to be careful about property. Gates should be closed or open, according to the land holder's wishes. If fences are crossed, they should be slipped under or crossed in some way to avoid stretching the wire or pulling out staples or putting weight on weak parts. Livestock should not be alarmed nor traps set that farm dogs or cats may get into. No shooting should be done near occupied buildings or near livestock or people working in fields—especially with rifles, from which glancing bullets may go whining off. One should avoid doing any kind of damage or giving cause for irritation. If anyone ever does have a mishap involving the land holder's property, he should go immediately to him, tell him about it, and offer to make good on any damage.

And, as an exercise in golden-ruling, a youngster might keep in mind that not all of the unfriendliness of certain land holders toward outsiders may be due to the land holders having been born cussed or having developed cussedness by choice. Some of it may be an outgrowth of years of provocation by the exploiting or trespassing public. There are people who have had so many unfortunate things happen to them that the public has become an affliction. They can tell enough about open gates, broken fences, fires due to carelessness, shot livestock, frightened or endangered families to make understandable why they find it hard to be nice to more strangers asking permission for this or that even when the strangers conduct themselves with complete gentlemanliness. It takes a lot of good behavior on the part of the majority to offset recklessness and wantonness on the part of the few.

*   *   *

The campaigning that local or national organizations carry on against littering our out-of-doors with trash has real justification behind it. When we see the slogan, "Don't be a litterbug," or its equivalent, it is not because someone is trying to infringe upon our personal liberties. Strong words about our littering being a national disgrace may be read in newspaper and magazine editorials and articles from one end of our country to the other. It is quite easy to gain the impression that our public manners lack something.

It is still easier to gain that impression by walking along the general run of American lake shores and stream banks and wooded places frequented by considerable numbers of people. I have in mind a public-owned body of water, partly marshy and partly lake-like, which has long been a "project" for an organization of several hundred people. Thousands of dollars have been expended in trying to improve its fishing, boating, and other recreational facilities. It has picnicking places, with tables and garbage barrels and signs tactfully asking people to be on good behavior. But some people still leave the shores messed up with paper, old clothes, cans, bottles, etc., and now and then someone makes a special contribution by dumping boxes of kitchen garbage or bales of newspapers into the water or engaging in bottle-smashing games.

Trappers, too, come in the category of people who can mess up the out-of-doors or leave it clean, young trappers as well as old ones. Usually, I feel no objection toward modest quantities of skinned carcasses of fur-bearers being left in the out-of-doors, returning their bones to the soil after contributing food for wild flesh-feeders. Many years ago, a party of trappers left a beautiful island in a northern Iowa marsh looking like a start on an ordinary small town dump except for a huge pile of muskrat carcasses. Now, nothing remains of the pile of carcasses but inconspicuous bone fragments scattered over the ground, but no one need search to see the old metal and glass, nor to question that it will last a long time to come.

Youngsters do not have to follow the bad examples of some of their elders just because bad examples can be found. Whether bad manners in the out-of-doors take the form of littering or shooting up signs or irresponsible conduct in other ways, young trappers do not have to do these things. In fact, it could be that *they* might set some good examples for their elders if they would. The views of a well-regarded young person are not always without influence on the outlook of older people.

One last bit of cautioning with regard to outdoor values and human attitudes: No one should let any desires to keep the out-of-doors clean lead to unfortunate extremes that destroy the very values we seek to preserve. I refer to the damage or destruction—in the name of development or landscaping or cleaning up—of wild places that are valuable in thickly settled communities chiefly because they are wild or because they offer the kinds of places that furbearers or game or song birds or any interesting wildlife must have in order to thrive or even, in many cases, to live at all.

Wild creatures live where they have suitable living conditions, and what is suitable differs with the adaptations of the species concerned. If we want creatures adapted to live on lawns, we will get them on lawns, but, if we want marsh creatures or woodland creatures or brushland creatures, we will not have them unless they have what they need. The down logs and hollow den trees of wooded stream banks and lake shores, the undergrowths of berry bushes and vines and wild flowers and tree saplings, the cattails and bulrushes and other natural coverings of marsh waters—these natural things should not be cleared away merely because they were not put there by the hand of man.

SELECTED REFERENCES

T HE FOLLOWING selection of references is intended to give the reader an idea of where to look if he wishes to consult some of the published background for this book. The references are mainly technical, and their selection, furthermore, is narrowed down to those that the reader should have some chance of finding, as in the larger university or governmental libraries of the United States and Canada.

I am first listing publications of my own authorship, insofar as the book is so largely based upon personal experience and field work:

Errington, Paul L.

1937. Food habits of Iowa red foxes during a drought summer. Ecology, Vol. 18, No. 1, pp. 53-61.

. . . . and Carolyn Storm Errington

1937. Experimental tagging of young muskrats for purposes of study. Journal of Wildlife Management, Vol 1, No. 3-4, pp. 49-61.

. . . .

1937. Habitat requirements of stream-dwelling muskrats. Transactions of the Second North American Wildlife Conference, pp. 411-416.

. . . .

1937. Observations on muskrat damage to corn and other crops in central Iowa. Journal of Agricultural Research, Vol. 57, No. 6, pp. 415-422.

. . . .

1939. Reactions of muskrat populations to drought. Ecology, Vol. 20, No. 2, pp. 168-186.

. . . .

1939. Observations on young muskrats in Iowa. Journal of Mammalogy, Vol. 20, No. 4, pp. 465-478.

. . . .

1940. Natural restocking of muskrat-vacant habitats. Journal of Wildlife Management, Vol. 4, No. 2, pp. 173-185.

. . . ., Frances Hamerstrom, and F. N. Hamerstrom, Jr.

1940. The great horned owl and its prey in north-central United States. Research Bulletin 277, Iowa Agricultural Experiment Station, pp. 757-850.

. . . .

1941. Versatility in feeding and population maintenance of the muskrat. Journal of Wildlife Management, Vol. 5, No. 1, pp. 68-89.

. . . .

1942. Observations on a fungus skin disease of Iowa muskrats. American Journal of Veterinary Research, Vol. 3, No. 7, pp. 195-201.

. . . .

1943. An analysis of mink predation upon muskrats in north-central United States. Research Bulletin 320, Iowa Agricultural Experiment Station, pp. 797-924.

. . . .

1944. Additional studies on tagged young muskrats. Journal of Wildlife Management, Vol. 8, No. 4, pp. 300-306.

. . . ., and Thomas G. Scott

1945. Reduction in productivity of muskrat pelts on an Iowa marsh through depredations of red foxes. Journal of Agricultural Research, Vol. 71, No. 4, pp. 137-148.

. . . .

1946. Predation and vertebrate populations. Quarterly Review of Biology, Vol. 21, No. 2-3, pp. 144-177, 221-245.

. . . .

1948. Environmental control for increasing muskrat production. Transactions of the Thirteenth North American Wildlife Conference, pp. 596-607.

. . . .

1951. Concerning fluctuations in populations of the prolific and widely distributed muskrat. American Naturalist, Vol. 85, No. 824, pp. 273-292.

....

1954. On the hazards of overestimating numerical fluctuations in studies of "cyclic" phenomena in muskrat populations. Journal of Wildlife Management, Vol. 18, No. 1, pp. 66-90.

....

1954. The special responsiveness of minks to epizootics in muskrat populations. Ecological Monographs, Vol. 24, No. 4, pp. 377-393.

....

1956. Factors limiting higher vertebrate populations. Science, Vol. 124, No. 3216, pp. 304-307.

In addition, I would particularly recommend two other papers based upon muskrat studies in Iowa.

Snead, I. Edwin

1950. A family live trap, handling cage, and associated techniques for muskrats. Journal of Wildlife Management, Vol. 14, No. 1, pp. 67-79.

Sprugel, George, Jr.

1951. Spring dispersal and settling activities of central Iowa muskrats. Iowa State College Journal of Science, Vol. 26, No. 1, pp. 71-84.

(Numerous progress reports on the Iowa muskrat studies have been written for the Quarterly Reports of the Iowa Cooperative Wildlife Research Unit. While these reports contain information not yet to be found in published form, the majority of at least the ones I wrote are now so out of date and incomplete and so difficult to get hold of that I do not think it would be worth while for many readers to try to consult them.)

Selected publications dealing with muskrats and their ways of life in parts of the north-central region other than Iowa:

Beer, James R., and Roland K. Meyer

1951. Seasonal changes in the endocrine organs and behavior patterns of the muskrat. Journal of Mammalogy, Vol. 32, No. 2, pp. 173-191.

Bellrose, Frank C.
   1950. The relationship of muskrat populations to various
         marsh and aquatic plants. Journal of Wildlife Man-
         agement, Vol. 14, No. 3, pp. 299-315.

........, and Louis G. Brown
   1941. The effect of fluctuating water levels on the muskrat
         population of the Illinois River Valley. Journal of
         Wildlife Management, Vol. 5, No. 2, pp. 206-212.

........, and Jessop B. Low
   1943. The influence of flood and low water levels on the
         survival of muskrats. Journal of Mammalogy, Vol. 24,
         No. 2, pp. 173-188.

Shanks, Charles E., and George C. Arthur
   1952. Muskrat movements and population dynamics in Mis-
         souri farm ponds and streams. Journal of Wildlife
         Management, Vol. 16, No. 2, pp. 138-148.

Selected publications dealing with harvesting muskrats for fur:

Aldous, Shaler E.
   1947. Muskrat trapping on Sand Lake National Wildlife
         Refuge, South Dakota. Journal of Wildlife Manage-
         ment, Vol. 11, No. 1, pp. 77-90.

Gashwiler, Jay S.
   1949. The effect of spring muskrat trapping on waterfowl in
         Maine. Journal of Wildlife Management, Vol. 13, No.
         2, pp. 183-188.

Mathiak, Harold A., and Arlyn F. Linde
   1954. Role of Refuges in Muskrat Management. Technical
         Wildlife Bulletin No. 10, Wisconsin Conservation De-
         partment, Madison, Wisconsin, 16 pp.

Selected publications dealing with serious diseases of muskrats:
Parker, R. R., Edward A. Steinhaus, Glenn M. Kohls, and William
L. Jellison
   1951. Contamination of natural waters and mud with
         Pasteurella tularensis and tularemia in beavers and
         muskrats in the Northwestern United States. National
         Institutes of Health Bulletin No. 193, U. S. Public
         Health Service. 61 pp.

Lord, G. H., A. C. Todd, and C. Kabat
  1956. Studies on Errington's disease in muskrats. I Pathological changes. American Journal of Veterinary Research, Vol. 17, No. 63, pp. 303-306.
........., ..., ..., and H. Mathiak
  1956. Studies on Errington's disease in muskrats. II Etiology. American Journal of Veterinary Research, Vol. 17, No. 63, pp. 307-310.

Selected references dealing more or less with muskrat environment and with ways of managing muskrat environment in behalf of wetland wildlife, including muskrats:

Addy, C. E., C. F. De La Barre, and D. W. Cardwell
  1942. Farm fish ponds. Bulletin of the Virginia Polytechnic Institute, (Blacksburg, Virginia) Vol. 35, No. 11, 45 pp.
........., and L. G. MacNamara
  1948. Waterfowl management on small areas. (In two parts, the first by Addy on ponds and marshes for waterfowl and the second by MacNamara on methods of pond and lake construction.) Wildlife Management Institute, Washington, D. C., 84 pp.

Davison, Verne E.
  1947. Farm fishponds for food and good land use. Farmers' Bulletin 1983, United States Department of Agriculture. 29 pp.

Martin, Alexander C.
  1953. Improving duck marshes by weed control. Circular 19, Fish and Wildlife Service, United States Department of the Interior. 49 pp.

Mathiak, Harold A., and Arlyn F. Linde
  1956. Studies on level ditching for marsh management. Technical Wildlife Bulletin No. 12. Wisconsin Conservation Department, Madison, Wisconsin. 49 pp.

McDonald, Malcolm E.
  1955. Causes and effects of a die-off of emergent vegetation. Journal of Wildlife Management, Vol. 19, No. 1, pp. 24-35.

Provost, Maurice W.
  1948. Marsh-blasting as a wildlife management technique. Journal of Wildlife Management, Vol. 12, No. 4, pp. 350-387.

Speirs, J. Murray
    1948. Summary of literature on aquatic weed control. Canadian Fish Culturist, Vol. 3, No. 4, pp. 20-32.

Selected publications dealing with muskrats and muskrat management of southern coastal marshes:

O'Neil, Ted.
    1949. The muskrat in the Louisiana coastal marshes. Louisiana Department of Wildlife and Fisheries, New Orleans, xii+152 pp.

Lay, Daniel W.
    1945. Muskrat investigations in Texas. Journal of Wildlife Management, Vol. 9, No. 1, pp. 56-76.
    ...., and Ted O'Neil
    1942. Muskrats on the Texas Coast. Journal of Wildlife Management, Vol. 6, No. 4, pp. 301-311.

Lynch, John J., Ted O'Neil, and Daniel W. Lay
    1947. Management significance of damage by geese and muskrats to Gulf Coast marshes. Journal of Wildlife Management, Vol. 11, No. 1, pp. 50-76.

Dozier, Herbert L.
    1947. Salinity as a factor in Atlantic Coast tidewater muskrat production. Transactions of the Twelfth North American Wildlife Conference, pp. 398-420.

    ....
    1948. Estimating muskrat populations by house count. Transactions of the Thirteenth North American Wildlife Conference, pp. 372-389.

    ....
    1953. Muskrat production and management. Circular 18, Fish and Wildlife Service, United States Department of the Interior. ii+42 pp.

There is now a substantial literature on the muskrat as an acclimated animal in the Old World, but most of this is in German, Swedish, Finnish, and Russian. Of the English-language publications on this subject, the two listed below should be as conveniently accessible to American readers as any:

Storer, Tracy I.
    1937. The muskrat as native and alien. Journal of Mammalogy, Vol. 18, No. 4, pp. 443-460.

. . . .

1938. The muskrat as native and alien: a chapter in the history of animal acclimatization. California Fish and Game, Vol. 24, No. 2, pp. 159-175.

The reader might also find it advantageous to look for papers on muskrats, etc., in back numbers of such periodicals as the Journal of Mammalogy and the Journal of Wildlife Management, both of which are widely distributed in North American science libraries. Wildlife Review, which is published by the United States Fish and Wildlife Service, is a most useful source of information on current literature on wildlife management, including muskrat management.

Finally, I may enthusiastically recommend for people interested in muskrats a book that has little about muskrats in it, but a book containing the best general treatment of wildlife ecology and management—or call it conservation—of which I know:

Allen, Durward L.
1954. Our wildlife legacy. Funk and Wagnalls, New York, x+422 pp.